A GUIDE TO

F. SCOTT FITZGERALD'S ST. PAUL

John J. Koblas

A GUIDE TO

F. SCOTT FITZGERALD'S ST. PAUL

John J. Koblas

Minnesota Historical Society Press

www.mnhs.org/mhspress

The Minnesota Historical Society Press is a member of the Association of American University Presses.

Printed in Canada.

10 9 8 7 6 5 4 3 2 1

∞ The paper used in this publication meets the minimum requirements of the American National Standard for Information Sciences—Permanence for Printed Library Materials, ANSI Z39.48-1984.

Photo p. 39 by Doug Ohman. All 1978 photographs by Alan Ominsky. Other pictures are from the collections of the Minnesota Historical Society.

International Standard Book Number 0-87351-513-7

Originally published as *F. Scott Fitzgerald in Minnesota* (1978), ISBN 0-87351-134-4

The Library of Congress has cataloged the 1978 edition as follows:

Koblas, John J. 1942–
 F. Scott Fitzgerald in Minnesota
(Minnesota historic sites pamphlet series; no. 18)
(Publications of the Minnesota Historical Society)
Includes bibliographical references.
 1. Fitzgerald, Francis Scott Key, 1896–1940—Homes and haunts—Minnesota. 2. Authors, American—20th century—Biography. 3. Minnesota—Biography.
 4. Historic buildings—Minnesota. 1. Title. II. Series.
 III. Series: Minnesota Historical Society. Publications.
PS3511.I9Z673
813'.5'2 [B]

78-21979

For Lynette, Stacy, Stephanie, John, and Sarah

A GUIDE TO
F. SCOTT FITZGERALD'S
ST. PAUL

ACKNOWLEDGMENTS

I am indebted to Alexander P. Clark, former curator of manuscripts in the Firestone Library at Princeton University, and to the many courteous librarians I besieged at the Minnesota Historical Society, the Hill Reference Library, the Minneapolis Public Library, and the St. Paul Public Library, especially its Highland Park Branch which houses an F. Scott Fitzgerald collection.

I am grateful to the following persons for granting interviews, access to materials, or freedom to wander about their facilities: Sister Mary Regina McCabe and the other good sisters of the Convent of the Visitation; John S. Fitch, school historian of St. Paul Academy; Father Clyde Eddy of St. Paul Seminary; Gene J. Marshall, manager of the White Bear Yacht Club; Margery Schneeman of the White Bear Area Historical Society; and Ethel Cline of the Fitzgerald residence at 599 Summit Avenue.

To the following helpful people I owe a very special tribute. Although some of their contributions are specifically acknowledged in the footnotes, each in his or her own way shared useful information—memories, research notes, an elusive fact, or perhaps a vital telephone number: Mrs. Richard Bertram, Raymond Burrington, Mary D. Cannon, Lew M. Cabos, Eric Carlson, Robert D. Clark, Jill Clayton, Everett Corbett, Mrs. John Farrington, William Fobes, Jr., Msgr. Francis Gilligan, Carolyn Gilman, Benjamin G. Griggs, Vince Guarnera, Theresa Gurney, Lloyd Hackl, Clark Hansen, Brooks Henderson, Keith Horning, Frank Hurley, Jr., Mr. and Mrs. Norris D. Jackson, Jeanette Kamman, Helen T. Katz, Mrs. Walter J. Kennedy, Mr. and Mrs. Andrew LaBarre, Mrs. Herbert L. Lewis, Harry Mackenhausen,

Margaret MacLaren, Mr. and Mrs. George Mairs, Elberta Matters, Marion Matters, Mrs. Daniel McCarthy, Patrick and Mary L. McQuillan, Diane Moellring, Thomond O'Brien, William O'Connell, Mr. and Mrs. Richardson B. Okie, Alan Ominsky, Jack Ramaley, Clifton and James Read, Frances J. Sains, Mrs. Carl T. Schuneman, Jr., Barbara Simpson, Phillip Stringer, Jean Ingersoll Summersby, Harry Svardahl, Mackey J. Thompson, Richard L. Tierney, Donald A. Wandrei, Joseph H. Watson, Stephen Weappa, Joseph A. West, William Westen, Mrs. Perry Wilson, Joseph M. Wise, John Withy, and Jack G. Young.

The completion of this booklet was made possible by a Minnesota Historical Society Research Grant made to the author in 1977. To the society's editors, June D. Holmquist, Jean A. Brookins, and especially Virginia L. Martin, I extend my thanks for guidance and cooperation.

Last, but in no way least, I wish to thank my uncle, John ("Yano") Hibbing, who long ago permitted a very small boy to ride with him in his delivery truck and thus discover for himself the streets, hills, and buildings of what I later learned were the St. Paul haunts of F. Scott Fitzgerald.

A GUIDE TO

F. SCOTT FITZGERALD'S ST. PAUL

INTRODUCTION

Ernest Hemingway wrote a short story in which he had a fictional F. Scott Fitzgerald observe, "The rich are different from you and me"—to which someone supposedly responded, "Yes, they have more money." The tale has been told and retold ever since. Their editor, Max Perkins, tried in vain to correct the facts: the exchange took place, he said, between Hemingway and a critic, and it was the critic who had the last word. But the story stuck, perhaps because this observation, with its mixture of envy, awe, admiration, and cynicism, so succinctly expressed Fitzgerald's attitude. That attitude was formed in St. Paul, where he grew up on the fringe of the city's most elegant residential area.

Fitzgerald was born in St. Paul in 1896. His association with the city can be divided into four periods—his debut from 1896 to 1899; his school days from 1908 to 1911; his frequent comings and goings from 1912 to 1919, while he was away in prep school, college, and the army; and the final curtain in 1921–22, when Scott and his wife Zelda left for the last time.[1]

The first part of this guidebook, "St. Paul Buildings in Fitzgerald's Life," features thirty-five of the buildings that Fitzgerald and his family lived in or frequented. They are arranged chronologically, so that readers may follow Fitzgerald's path through the city. The second part, "Fitzgerald Buildings in St. Paul," provides brief descriptions of these thirty-five structures and of seventy-one others that have connections to the author's friends and relatives. They are organized by street name and keyed to the maps on pages 58, 59, and 60, to facilitate walking and driving tours. Only twenty-one

3

of the 106 places described here have been destroyed.

It is perhaps odd that Fitzgerald, who traveled halfway around the globe as an adult, should see so little of his home state. Except for frequent excursions to White Bear and Bald Eagle lakes, located in the St. Paul suburb of White Bear Lake, his travels in Minnesota were restricted to brief trips during the summers of 1909 and 1916 to Hastings, Frontenac, Duluth, and Brainerd. These trips are easily summarized.[2]

Scott's first recorded safari beyond the St. Paul–White Bear orbit occurred in June 1909, when he and his friend Wharton Smith pedaled their bicycles to Hastings and back. Two other trips occurred in July. Scott spent ten days in the village of Frontenac, a "dignified" summer resort village since the post–Civil War era nestled on the bluff of the Mississippi River near Red Wing. There he was the invited guest of the Pierce Butler family, staying in a cottage associated with the Frontenac Hotel. By sheer coincidence, Jean Ingersoll, a St. Paul friend, was also enjoying a month's vacation with her parents at Frontenac. Jean, Scott, and some of the local youngsters got together to explore the deep woods, the bluffs that seemed like miniature mountains, and the sandy beaches along the river, where they congregated to exchange meager sexual information or swap stories about the kids back home.[3]

Before July expired, Scott accompanied his mother to Duluth. Apparently mother and son intended to go abroad, but the boy came down with appendicitis, and they were forced to remain in Duluth until he recovered. He must have done so quickly, for his ledger for July reads: "Started abroad with mother. Appendicitus [sic] in Duluth. Down the great lakes. Revisited Buffalo."[4]

Illness seems also to have been involved in Fitzgerald's only recorded visit to Brainerd, a resort community on the Mississippi River 130 miles north of St. Paul. He went there in July 1916 on what he cryptically referred to only as an "ill-fated health trip." It is known that Scott returned to St. Paul during the winter before suffering from what was believed to be malaria, which was then endemic at Princeton University, where he was in his sophomore year. Nothing more is known of the Brainerd excursion, which his parents may have hoped would be beneficial to his recovery from what was later determined to be a mild case of tuberculosis rather than malaria.[5]

But most of the Minnesota sites associated with the author are found in St. Paul, the city where he spent his boyhood and wrote the first novel that brought him fame. They are concentrated in an area approximately twelve blocks square, stretching from the stately Cathedral of St. Paul west along Summit Avenue as far as Grotto, north to Selby, and south to Fairmount. Fitzgerald's St. Paul encompasses parts of the Summit, Ramsey Hill, Crocus Hill, and Woodland Park districts of the city.

Edward and Mary ("Mollie") McQuillan Fitzgerald were comfortable, but they were not rich by the standards of Summit Avenue, the most prestigious street in the city. Like their houses, the Fitzgeralds stood a little at the edge of society: they occupied a slightly precarious social position and possessed a certain genteel shabbiness.[6]

Scott was born on Laurel Avenue as the nineteenth century came to a close. His mother was the eldest child of Philip F. McQuillan, an Irish immigrant who

Phillip Francis McQuillan, grandfather of F. Scott Fitzgerald, about 1890, and the McQuillan Block, Wabasha and Third Street, about 1870

had made a fortune in the wholesale grocery business. Mollie, who was regarded as gauche and eccentric, had no interest in society except to help further her children's ambitions. Edward, as it turned out, contributed to the marriage his good breeding, charm, and elegant manners, but little in the way of financial support.[7]

At the time Scott was born, his father had a small wicker-furniture business. The firm failed in the 1897 depression and Edward accepted a job in 1898 as a soap salesman for Procter and Gamble, moving his wife and two-year-old son first to Buffalo, then Syracuse, then back to Buffalo, New York. He was fired from his job in 1908, and the family (enlarged in 1901 with the birth of a daughter, Annabel) returned to the security of St. Paul and the McQuillan family home and fortune. Probably through the good offices of Louisa A. McQuillan, his wealthy mother-in-law, Edward obtained a position as a broker in the wholesale grocery business. In actuality, the ineffectual, charming, alcoholic Fitzgerald never worked again. The charge, "If it weren't for [Grandfather McQuillan] where would we be now?" echoed around the Fitzgerald house and underlined the failure of Scott's father.[8]

F. Scott Fitzgerald and his mother on Laurel Avenue, 1897.
A neighbor, Edith Brill, took the photograph.

Scott was a precocious eleven-year-old when the Fitzgeralds returned to St. Paul. His was a restless family. Moving seemed to be an almost annual event for them. When they lived in the East, they seemed to have no fixed neighborhood, but when they returned to St. Paul—although they moved just as often—their various homes were all within the confines of an area of about twelve square blocks near Summit Avenue. Scott for the first time experienced the relative stability of residing within a single definable community and having a secure circle of friends. And he was exposed to the trappings of great wealth. He mingled with children whose surnames were often the same as the streets upon which they lived and played—Griggs, Mackubin, Hersey—the legacy of wealthy and eminent fathers and grandfathers.[9]

The elder Fitzgeralds did not mingle in this society, but Mollie saw to it that Scott met the right people. He was enrolled in the dancing class and prep school to which St. Paul's elite sent their children. He became part of the group that was invited to dances at Summit

The costume party celebrating the end of Professor Baker's dancing class at Ramaley Hall, 1910. Scott Fitzgerald is in the top row, far right.

Avenue homes, patronized the University Club, went to bobsled parties at the Town and Country Club, and sailed and swam at the White Bear Yacht Club.[10]

In both Fitzgerald's fiction and in his personal life, money and social position are recurrent themes and unresolved dilemmas. The mixed and shifting attitudes he held must have been born in the ambivalence of his own youthful life and experiences in St. Paul. Perhaps it was this ambivalence that gave Fitzgerald both his lifelong sense of insecurity and what Malcolm Cowley has called the "double vision" that pervades his fiction. "It was as if all his novels described a big dance to which he had taken . . . the prettiest girl," Cowley wrote, "and as if at the same time he stood outside the ballroom, a little Midwestern boy with his nose to the glass, wondering how much the tickets cost and who paid for the music."[11]

Fitzgerald and some friends at a photo parlor, using his props, about 1917. Left to right: Helen Floan, Sidney Strong, Grace Warner, Fitzgerald, Lucius P. Ordway, Jr.

Although Fitzgerald called St. Paul his home from 1908 until 1922, he was often away—at boarding school, at Princeton University, in the army, and in New York City. In this period he turned back to his home town for refuge and surcease. Hurt and determined when Zelda broke their engagement in 1919, he decided to become a successful novelist, and going home, he completed *This Side of Paradise*. Later, when Zelda was pregnant, the city was haven once again: "when our child was to be born we played safe and went home to St. Paul," he said.[12]

After he and Zelda left in 1922, seeking bigger and brighter lights, he never returned. Years later he wrote to

F. Scott and Zelda Fitzgerald were living at Dellwood in September 1921, when this picture was taken, about one month before Scottie was born.

Marie Hersey Hamm: "I no longer regard St. Paul as my home any more than the eastern seaboard or the Riviera. This is said with no disloyalty but simply because after all my father was an easterner and I went East to college and I never did quite adjust myself to those damn Minnesota winters. I was always freezing my cheeks, being a rotten skater, etc.—though many events there will always fill me with a tremendous nostalgia."[13]

Fitzgerald drew on his St. Paul experiences, as he drew on everything in his life, for his fiction. The stories most clearly based in St. Paul are those featuring Basil Duke Lee, for which the writer's own adolescence is the rather transparent model. "The Scandal Detectives," "The Captured Shadow," "Forging Ahead," and "A Night at the Fair" all included thinly disguised people, places, and events from his childhood—the Ames's backyard, Cecil Read's attic, the Minnesota State Fair, and Scott's theatrical ventures with the Elizabethan Dramatic Club. Other clearly identifiable St. Paul settings are the Winter Carnival, an annual civic event which he used in "The Ice Palace," and the White Bear Yacht Club, which appeared in "Winter Dreams."[14]

But the most famous description of Fitzgerald's Midwest is the one offered by his transplanted midwestern hero, Nick Carraway, in *The Great Gatsby,* which is usually considered Fitzgerald's finest book:

> One of my most vivid memories is coming back West from prep school and later from college at Christmas time. Those who went farther than Chicago would gather in the old dim Union Street Station at six o'clock of a December evening, with a few Chicago friends, already caught up into their own holiday gayeties, to bid them a hasty good-by. I remember the fur coats of the girls returning from Miss This-or-That's and the chatter of frozen breath and the hands waving overhead as we caught sight of old acquaintances, and the matchings of invitations: "Are you going to the Ordways'? The Herseys'? The Schultzes'?" and the long green tickets clasped tight in our gloved hands. And last the murky yellow cars of the Chicago, Milwaukee & St. Paul railroad looking cheerful as Christmas itself on the tracks beside the gate.
>
> When we pulled out into the winter night and the real snow, our snow, began to stretch out beside us and twinkle against the windows, and the dim lights of small Wisconsin stations moved by, a sharp, wild brace came suddenly into the air. We

drew in deep breaths of it as we walked back from dinner through the cold vestibules, unutterably aware of our identity with this country for one strange hour, before we melted indistinguishably into it again.

That's my Middle West—not the wheat or the prairies or the lost Swede towns, but the thrilling returning trains of my youth, and the street lamps and the sleigh bells in the frosty dark and the shadows of holly wreaths thrown by lighted windows on the snow.[15]

The Midwest of Fitzgerald's experience and of his fiction is "centered on Summit Avenue." Summit forms a spine for what was the most fashionable neighborhood in St. Paul. The avenue begins at its intersection with Selby where the majestic Cathedral of St. Paul rises. For some six blocks it angles southwesterly until, near Western Avenue, it crooks its elbow, then sweeps westward to its termination at the Mississippi River, four and a half miles away.[16]

Summit Avenue near Western, looking east, about 1900

Clustered around the most elegant, eastern end of the avenue are Summit Court and Crocus, Grand, and Ramsey hills; the area was designated the Historic Hill District and placed on the National Register of Historic Places in 1976. To the north is Woodland Park, which was added to the register in 1978. In the 1980s these neighborhoods became the scene of much rejuvenation, with many middle-income people, particularly young people, buying and rehabilitating the big, beautiful, old homes. According to one architectural historian, "St. Paul's Summit Avenue stands as the best-preserved American example of the Victorian monumental residential boulevard." And he notes that the "panorama of the avenue remains little altered from the 1920s." Although Summit and its environs are no longer the exclusive property of the rich, it is this sense of preservation and renewal that so impresses both tourists and natives, who enjoy strolling, jogging, bicycling, and driving along this thoroughfare.[17]

It is still possible to revisit the streets of Fitzgerald's St. Paul. With a little imagination, one can re-create in fancy how these neighborhoods looked when F. Scott Fitzgerald was young. Elegant homes, almost unaltered by time, still adorn the picturesque bluff overlooking the Mississippi River Valley, and the seemingly alien world of the modern city stretches out below like an immense carpet. In the midst of these buildings of a bygone era one can hear the whispering voices of yesterday, when a boy wore Eton collars, rode the electric streetcars to White Bear Lake, and dreamed of being a famous writer. A walk though the streets of Fitzgerald's St. Paul allows one to recapture, for a little while, the past of the early twentieth century, gain insights into the young author's world, and sense the ambience and the ambivalence that he recorded so well.

FITZGERALD'S LIFE IN ST. PAUL

P. F. McQUILLAN HOUSE
249 East Tenth Street
(renumbered 397 East Tenth Street in 1881)
3, MAP B

Philip F. and Louisa Allen McQuillan, F. Scott Fitzgerald's maternal grandparents, built one of the more fashionable dwellings in St. Paul's Lowertown in 1872 or 1873. The elegant home symbolized the meteoric rise of "P. F.," as he was called, from the status of Irish immigrant in 1834 to prominence as one of St. Paul's wealthiest businessmen in the 1870s. He arrived from Galena, Illinois, in 1857, found employment with a grocery firm, and within two years established his own small retail grocery store on which he founded his multimillion-dollar wholesale food business. He also built a four-story building on the corner of Third and Sibley streets, and he bought a substantial stone building (later known as the McQuillan Block), which had been built by Joseph L. Forepaugh at the corner of Third and Wabasha streets.[1]

P. F. McQuillan house, 249 East Tenth St., about 1905

The McQuillan house boasted a cupola, as did many others of that era, but it was the unusual walkway that attracted curious St. Paulites out on Sunday strolls. Instead of the usual gravel paths, the walk was composed of seashells and bordered with conches.[2]

P. F. McQuillan died in 1877 at the age of forty-three, a victim of Bright's disease, leaving a personal fortune of over a quarter of a million dollars. Louisa remained in the mansion with her five children, the oldest of whom was Mollie, who would become the mother of F. Scott Fitzgerald. In 1893, when the McQuillans moved to Laurel Terrace on Summit Hill, the Tenth Street house was sold to Luther Hospital and converted into that institution's headquarters. The once-fashionable Lowertown became the city's business and warehouse district. Parts of it have been obliterated by the construction of Interstate 94. The McQuillan house and many others have vanished from the St. Paul scene.[3]

F. SCOTT FITZGERALD BIRTHPLACE
481 Laurel Avenue
44, MAP A

In this three-story brick apartment building, Mollie Fitzgerald gave birth at 3:30 p.m., September 24, 1896, to a ten-pound, six-ounce baby boy. He was delivered by Dr. Benjamin H. Ogden—one of twenty-eight professional men in the immediate neighborhood—and was christened Francis Scott Key Fitzgerald for one of his father's more illustrious ancestors. The family had moved into the San Mateo Flats, as the building for unknown reasons was called, and setting a pattern that the Fitzgerald family and Scott himself would repeat, they did not live there very long.[4]

Scott was baptized by Father John T. Harrison on October 6 in the Cathedral of St. Paul, now located where Summit Avenue begins. His sponsors were Philip McQuillan, an uncle, and Emilie Harden. When he was less than a month old, Scott was taken on his first outing to John Lambert's notions at 500 Laurel and to William H. Kane's grocery at the same intersection at Mackubin, a short walk of a half block. At eight months, he had learned to crawl; at one year he had

Fitzgerald birthplace, 481 Laurel, about 1964

cut six teeth; and shortly afterwards he spoke his first word: "Up."[5]

Scott was not as robust a baby as his impressive birth weight would suggest. During his first fourteen months of life, his health was repeatedly threatened by colic and colds. In December 1897 he suffered a severe case of bronchitis. "A specialist was summoned," he wrote in his ledger years later, "but as his advice was not followed the child pulled through."[6]

By 1897 Edward Fitzgerald's wicker-furniture manufacturing business, the American Rattan and Willow Works, was in serious financial trouble. Within a year the company fell victim to the crippling depression that had struck the nation, and its doors were closed. Jobs in St. Paul were scarce, as they were in all parts of the country at that time, but the senior Fitzgerald secured a position in Buffalo, New York, as a traveling salesman for Procter and Gamble. The Fitzgerald family moved there in April 1898. The next nine years would be spent in that city, except for a brief period in Syracuse, trips to neighboring states, and one visit to the McQuillan home on Summit Avenue in St. Paul in 1899. They would not return to St. Paul until Scott was eleven years old and already dreaming of becoming a writer.[7]

F. Scott Fitzgerald's birthplace on Laurel Avenue still stands, although it has undergone extensive interior remodeling. In 2004 the building was designated a Literary Landmark by the Friends of Libraries USA.

LOUISA McQUILLAN HOUSE
623 Summit Avenue
85, MAP A

Louisa McQuillan, F. Scott Fitzgerald's grandmother, moved into her newly constructed house in 1897. She had purchased the property in 1893 from nurseryman William West for $35,000; it consisted of six adjacent lots, three fronting on Summit and three on Portland.[8]

Louisa McQuillan house, 623 Summit, about 1910

As a baby Fitzgerald was often taken to visit his grandmother during the short time she lived here. After he moved with his parents to Buffalo, New York, he accompanied his mother, who was no doubt lonesome for her family, on a last visit to this McQuillan house in 1899 when he was only two and a half years old. In later years Scott recalled the mansion, perhaps more clearly as a continuing presence in the neighborhood rather than as his grandmother's home.

Mrs. McQuillan sold the Victorian house in 1899 to Albert P. Warren for $18,000. She then moved into the Aberdeen Hotel at the corner of Dayton and Virginia—the first of four moves she would make before her death in 1913.

The three-story brick residence still stands at the intersection of Summit and Dale.

LOUISA McQUILLAN RESIDENCE
286 and 294 Laurel Avenue
(known as Laurel Terrace and Riley Row)
40, MAP A

In 1908 after Scott's father Edward was fired from his sales job with Procter and Gamble in Buffalo, New York, the family returned to St. Paul in July. Scott, age eleven, and his sister Annabel, seven, were welcomed into their Grandmother McQuillan's apartment at 294 Laurel, while their parents moved in temporarily with John A. Fulton, an old family friend who lived a few blocks away at 239 Summit Avenue. Edward Fitzgerald secured a position as a broker in the grocery business, but it was clear that the McQuillan fortune was the major source of the family's income.[9]

Mrs. Fitzgerald was determined that her children should not be dragged down by their father's failure. Scott was enrolled at St. Paul Academy and in Professor William H. Baker's dancing class, where he met the children who would be his "crowd' for the next ten years; a few would remain friends for much longer. But the

Laurel Terrace, also known as "Riley Row," 286–294 Laurel, 1978. This row house also has apartments fronting on Nina.

Fitzgeralds, like their houses, were always a little on the periphery of wealth, and as one biographer writes, Scott grew up "desiring with all the intensity of his nature to succeed according to [society's] standard and always conscious of hovering socially on the edge of it, alternating between assertion and uncertainty because of his acute awareness that his foothold was unsure."[10]

In April 1909 Grandmother McQuillan traveled abroad, and Scott's parents joined their children at 294 Laurel. Five months later the reunited family would move into their own place on Holly Avenue.[11]

Riley Row—named for its builder, William C. Riley—was built about 1884 of brownstone and red pressed brick following a three-story town house plan popular in its day. Ten years later Louisa McQuillan moved in for the first time, living at 286 Laurel from 1894 to 1896.[12]

CONVENT OF THE VISITATION

720 Fairmount Avenue

10, MAP A

On pleasant days Mollie Fitzgerald often visited the convent where she and her sisters Clara and Annabel had attended school, taking young Scott with her to show him off. Mollie had lost three children—two daughters before Scott was born and a third when he was four. She was, moreover, deeply disappointed in her husband, who never really worked again after losing his job as a soap salesman and who drank too much. Thus she lavished attention but little discipline on her only son. When they called at the Convent of the Visitation, she would urge him to recite, often something he had written, for the admiring nuns. She also encouraged him to sing for visitors, and later Scott would write wincingly of himself, "He used to sing for company—God!"[13]

Convent of the Visitation, 720 Fairmount, 1929

The Convent of the Visitation was established in 1873 in Lowertown on Somerset Avenue (the avenue no longer exists), then moved to Robert and University, and in 1913 to Fairmount and Grotto, where it remained until 1966 when further expansion made it necessary to relocate on Dodd Road in Mendota.[14]

Grandfather McQuillan had contributed financial support to the convent, and many years later Mollie's granddaughter, Scottie Fitzgerald, was baptized there with Father Joe Barron as godfather and Alexandra (Mrs. Charles O.) Kalman as godmother.

ST. PAUL ACADEMY
25 North Dale Street

7, MAP A

Scott was enrolled in St. Paul Academy, a preparatory school, in the fall of 1908, the year the Fitzgeralds returned to St. Paul. At first, he was cocky and fresh and not particularly popular with his classmates. The school magazine, *Now and Then,* quickly labeled him as the boy who knew "How to Run the School," and asked if there were not someone who would "poison Scotty or find some means to shut his mouth."[15]

He tended to be an exhibitionist—a trait his mother encouraged. He was the school's star debater (no one had found a way of shutting him up, wrote one biographer). He was imaginative, quickly inventing such amusements as the Scandal Detectives and the Goosrah club, a society for the cruelty to animals, the mock wedding, and a secret language. He played football, baseball, and basketball, usually on the second and third teams, but he was not good at sports. His first ledger entry for September 1908 read: "The Summit Football team. He [*Fitzgerald*] was Captain. One [*sic*] one, lost one and tied one. . . . Broke my ribs on St. Paul Academy team." Two years later he wrote, "Third and last year at the S.P.A. Played on the Summits. End and punter. Missed kick in crucial game."[16]

St. Paul Academy students, 25 North Dale, 1916

The grim determination with which he pursued athletics despite failure and humiliation (he weighed only 138 pounds in 1911) stemmed from his romantic vision of the heroic athlete. Football and the glamor of the gridiron provided material for his fiction. When he was fourteen he wrote a short story about a "light-haired stripling" who singlehandedly won a football game for his team. A Princeton football star was his model for Allenby, the hero in *This Side of Paradise*. As an adult, Fitzgerald often coped with insomnia by fantasizing about his heroics on the football field.

In his second year at the academy in 1909, Scott broke into print with his first published story, "The Mystery of the Raymond Mortgage," which appeared in *Now and Then*. In later years he recalled the excitement of his literary debut and his anxiety over its effect on his classmates. He published three more stories in the school magazine during the next two years—"Reade, Substitute Right Half," "A Debt of Honor," and "The Room With the Green Blinds."[17]

He also became a playwright. A children's production at the academy of a comedy entitled "A Regular Fix" so inspired Scott that he sat down and wrote "The Girl from the Lazy J," the first of four plays he would author for the Elizabethan Dramatic Club, an amateur group organized by Elizabeth Magoffin and named for her.[18]

Scott's grades at the academy were not impressive. He was often reprimanded for inattention and for scribbling plot outlines behind the covers of his textbooks. His poor scholastic record reflected the time he spent on extracurricular activities and his indifferent study habits. In 1911 the Fitzgeralds decided to send him to Newman School, a Catholic preparatory institution near Hackensack, New Jersey.

The St. Paul Academy, which had been an outgrowth of the Barnard School for Boys, was originally housed in the old Nushka Club building on Western Avenue next to the Angus Hotel. It moved to a new yellow brick building at 25 North Dale in 1904. Although the upper school moved to 1712 Randolph in 1916, the junior school remained at the Dale address until 1931, when it was moved to a new building at 718 Portland Avenue. In 1968 St. Paul Academy and Summit School merged into a single coeducational institution with two campuses, the upper school at 1712 Randolph and the lower school at 1150 Goodrich Avenue. The modest little brick building at the corner of Dale and Portland now houses a social service agency.[19]

GEORGE R. FINCH HOUSE
245 Summit Avenue
64, MAP A

Scott liked girls and they generally liked him. The year the Fitzgeralds returned to St. Paul, Scott, not quite twelve, was recovering from an unhappy case of puppy love he had suffered in Buffalo, New York. He was soon immersed in an "affair," as he termed it in his ledger entry for July 1908, with Violet Stockton, a young southerner who was visiting her aunt, Mrs. George R. Finch, for the summer. It was a mercurial romance. A quarrel began when Scott and a friend snatched away from Violet a little booklet on "flirting by signs." Angry and embarrassed, she quickly resolved never to see him again. The couple patched things up enough for Violet to give Scott a box of candy for his birthday on September 24, the day she left St. Paul and Scott's life for good.[20]

The boy wrote a seven-page "story of Violet Stockton" in his "Thoughtbook," ending with the melancholy notation five days after her departure that "Not much has happened since Violet went away."

The Finch house, which was built in 1882 and designed by A. M. Radcliffe, still stands guard at the brink of Summit Avenue.

Finch house, 245 Summit, 1978

F. SCOTT FITZGERALD RESIDENCES

514 Holly Avenue
33, MAP A
509 Holly Avenue
32, MAP A
499 Holly Avenue
31, MAP A

In September 1909, when Scott was thirteen, the Fitzgerald family moved out of Grandmother McQuillan's
apartment in Riley Row and took occupancy of a duplex
at 514 Holly Avenue. The new home afforded Scott more
privacy for his writing. His mother went abroad in the
summer of 1910 while Scott—and presumably Annabel—
stayed with Grandmother McQuillan. He became for a
time "desperately holy," attended St. Mary's Sunday
school, and received his first communion.[21]

The next September, in what seems to have been an
almost annual event, the family packed up and moved
again across the street into "Shotwell's house," a row
house at 509 Holly.
Stuart B. Shotwell
had been struck
and killed by a car
on May 22, 1910,
and the youthful
Fitzgerald had been
an eyewitness. (A
manslaughter
charge brought
against the young
woman driver was
subsequently
dropped by the

Fitzgerald residence, 514 Holly, 1978

family.) Scott became an "inveterate author," started
smoking, and acquired his first pair of long trousers and
a more profound interest in the opposite sex.[22]

In September 1911 Scott prepared for two moves:
the family rented a house at 499 Holly—their third

home on this street in as many years—and Scott planned to make a "new start" at Newman School in New Jersey. His years at St. Paul Academy had been singularly disappointing, and his family thought the Catholic school, where he would be "forced" to study, would be beneficial.[23]

Before he left for New Jersey, he and his friends had one last fling. They attended the Minnesota State Fair, where they met up with some "chickens" (fast girls) and rode the roller coaster. This was the summer that he and Richard ("Tubby") Washington began picking up such girls, and they would occasionally get, as they imagined, very drunk on a bottle of drugstore sherry.[24]

The three-story stone residence at 509 Holly, one of three connected town houses (505, 507, and 509), was designed by architect James Chisholm and constructed in 1887. The residences at 509 and 514 still stand, although the latter has been altered. The one at 499 Holly has been razed.[25]

Fitzgerald residence, 509 Holly, 1978

RAMALEY HALL

664–668 Grand Avenue

19, MAP A

In December 1909 Mrs. George E. (Janey MacLaren) Ingersoll organized a dancing class at Ramaley Hall. Mollie Fitzgerald enrolled thirteen-year-old Scott among the able, but not necessarily willing, pupils. The dancing master was Professor William H. Baker, an apple-shaped little man with a balding head and gray-white moustache, who worked summers as a bartender at the White Bear Yacht Club.[26]

The classes were held on Saturday afternoons in Ramaley Hall's pink and white ballroom. Among the approximately forty pupils, twenty of each sex, were children who bore the names of well-known St. Paul families—Ames, Armstrong, Bigelow, Boardman, Griggs, Hersey, Ingersoll, Jackson, Read, and Schurmeier. Until Scott left the city forever, these were the people with whom he would associate.

The girls were required to wear pretty dresses and petite slippers to class, while their less-than-enthusiastic partners sported serge suits, starched Eton collars, Windsor ties, black patent-leather shoes, and white cotton gloves.

Ramaley Hall, 664 Grand Avenue, 1956

The class continued into a second term in 1910. By then there were signs of rebellion among the boys. They circulated a petition to get a friend into the school and another requesting that they be taught more popular dances. A little later some of them refused to do the Grand March. Others, including Scott, executed the march, but "mushed it up every which way," forcing Baker to discontinue its performance.

In April an annual cotillion concluded the dancing class season and the brief struggle of wills. Each child dressed in a silly costume and took part in the fun and games.

Ramaley's Liquor Store and a parking lot now occupy part of the site of the former hall, which has been razed.

MRS. BACKUS' SCHOOL FOR GIRLS
580–590 Holly Avenue
36, MAP A

Mrs. Backus' School for Girls, housed in Oak Hall, was a private institution for young women attended by the daughters of many Summit Avenue families. Its principal

Riders at Oak Hall, 580–590 Holly, 1907

was Carrie H. Backus, and its manager was J. Clinton Backus. Advertisements for the school claimed that "St. Paul is the educational center of the Northwest, and the healthiest city in the world," and asked, "Why not send your daughter here?"[27]

Scott attended many dances at Oak Hall, including one to which he escorted Margaret Armstrong, one of his boyhood sweethearts. Of the four plays he wrote for the Elizabethan Dramatic Club, the second, "The Captured Shadow," was presented at Mrs. Backus' School on August 23, 1912. As usual, Scott was among the actors, playing the role of a burglar.

Oak Hall has been converted into an apartment complex, but it retains much of its former appearance.

CHARLES W. AMES HOUSE
501 Grand Hill
22, MAP A

The backyard of this house drew youngsters from all over the neighborhood to play with Theodore Ames, who was about Fitzgerald's age. Scott's memories of the yard were vivid, and he later used it as part of the setting for a Basil Duke Lee story, "The Scandal Detectives." Fitzgerald described the yard as having a "child's quality," with flowers, dogs, and brown patches where the grass had been worn away by the children's play. There was a three-story tree house in a large tree; its lowest platform accommodated about eight children, but only a few in the inner circle knew of the existence of its highest secret platform.[28]

At the time Scott knew the Ames family, Theodore's father was the general manager of the West Publishing Company, a major publisher of lawbooks. He was also the president of the St. Paul Institute of Arts and Sciences, which he had helped to found in 1908.

The well-maintained house still sits on Grand Hill. The backyard looks much as it did when Scott and his friends were growing up.

Ames house, 501 Grand Hill, 1978

EDWARD L. HERSEY HOUSE
475 Summit Avenue
78, MAP A

Throughout his St. Paul years, Scott was anything but a stranger to the well-constructed, imposing stone residence of E. L. Hersey, a wealthy lumberman. The boy met Marie Hersey almost immediately after the Fitzgeralds returned to St. Paul in 1908. The children were in dancing class together, were given to crushes on one another in their younger years, and became good friends as they grew up. In 1910 Scott recorded in his "Thoughtbook" that Marie had written him a love letter. The following February he revealed that he had deserted Alida Bigelow and now had "two new crushes. To wit—Margaret Armstrong and Marie Hersey." Marie was the prettiest, Margaret the best talker, he wrote.[29]

As Scott and Marie matured, so did their friend-ship. With Marie he attended many of Summit Hill's social events, including a party in the home of Louis Hill. The two friends also took in cultural events to-gether and exchanged letters after they went away to school. In December 1916 Marie visited Scott at Prince-ton to see the Triangle Club's theatrical production which he had helped to write. On at least one occasion after the acceptance of *This Side of Paradise* by Charles Scribner's Sons, publishers, Scott got drunk during a visit to Marie's home.[30]

The Hersey house, designed by George Wirth and built in 1883, has changed relatively little since the days when Scott was a frequent visitor there.

Hersey house, 475 Summit, about 1900

WILLIAM J. DEAN HOUSE
415 Summit Avenue
74, MAP A

The teenaged Scott found another good friend in Elisa-beth Dean, the daughter of a St. Paul wholesaler. He could confide in her, and he would often go to her with his problems, particularly about his love life. Scott was charmed by many young women as he was growing up. His flirtations fluctuated on an almost daily basis, and he was always making lists (divided by sex) of people he liked best, at the top of which could generally be found Marie Hersey, Alida Bigelow, and Margaret Armstrong.

To Elisabeth the thirteen-year-old Scott confessed his strong attraction to Margaret, calling her the most interesting person he had ever met (he would one day tell Elisabeth the same thing about Zelda Sayre). Elisabeth attempted to help Scott win Margaret, but in the end he lost out to his rival, Reuben Warner.[31]

Former state governor William R. Marshall built this two-story dwelling in the early 1880s, but it is not certain that he ever lived in it. Edwin W. Winter, later president of the Northern Pacific Railroad, owned the property in 1882. Elisabeth's father, William J. Dean, vice president and treasurer of Nicols, Dean and Gregg (wholesale iron, steel, and heavy hardware), acquired the property in 1907 and made general improvements, including the addition of a new porch and a bay window. It is possible that the beautiful Federal fanlighted doorway was installed at that time.[32]

Dean house, 415 Summit, 1978

C. MILTON GRIGGS HOUSE
365 Summit Avenue
72, MAP A

During his boyhood Scott spent many hours in the home of his friend Benjamin Griggs, the son of a prosperous St. Paul wholesaler and a fellow pupil at St. Paul Academy and in Professor Baker's dancing class. A vacant lot beside Ben's house served as a playground, a field for aspiring gridiron greats, or a baseball diamond. It was at a Saturday night party in this house in 1911 that Scott lost his childhood sweetheart, Margaret Armstrong, to his old friend and nemesis, Reuben Warner.[33]

Scott and Ben did not attend the same eastern schools. It is known, however, that they met again at least once more in the winter of 1921–22 when Scott

Griggs house, 365 Summit, 1978

and Zelda were part of a large bobsledding party that started from the University Club.

The stately Queen Anne house, designed by James Knox Taylor, a partner of Cass Gilbert, was built in 1891 by Mrs. Jacob W. Bass. In 1903 Mrs. Bass, her son, and her daughter-in-law exchanged houses with the Griggs family, and Griggs, sometime after that, added the "striking but inappropriate" Ionic front portico that survives to this day.

WILLIAM CECIL READ HOUSE
449 Portland Avenue
53, MAP A

Read house, 449 Portland, 1978

Cecil Read was one of Scott's closest companions as a boy and young man, and the Read house at 449 Portland was a favorite place for the neighborhood youngsters to assemble. One of its big attractions was its third-floor ballroom. Scott's youthful plays were produced in this room. Two of the clubs Scott initiated, the Scandal Detectives and the Goosrah, were also begun there. Many of Scott's friends, the clubs, and the events and activities they generated found their way into his fiction, particularly into his Basil Duke Lee stories. The day the boys "went after" Reuben Warner, a friend and rival of Scott's, resulted in the very real police calling upon the Fitzgerald family and Scott, ace detective, retiring from the profession. He later used the affair in his short story entitled "The Scandal Detectives."[34]

Cecil and several of the others in that "close little group"—Robert D. ("Bob") Clark, Paul Ballion, McNeil V. ("Mac") Seymour—went to Central High School instead of St. Paul Academy. Cecil and Scott were reunited at Princeton, where Cecil was one year behind Fitzgerald.

Scott brought him into the prestigious Cottage Club there.[35]

Cecil and Emily Lucile Weed were married in 1927. Several years later, when there had been no contact with Scott for a long time, a gift arrived for the Reads. It was a sterling silver plate with this inscription: "To Cecil on the occasion of his marriage in remembrance of 1000 misdeeds—Scott."

William Cecil Read, who owned a real estate, insurance, and mortgage loan company, died in 1909. The family moved to 442 Summit in 1911, then to 123 Nina, and in 1914 to 313 Laurel. "We were gypsies . . . uprooted by father's death," wrote Clifton Read, Cecil's brother. The Portland Avenue house was designed by Cass Gilbert and built in the 1880s for Cyrus H. Kellogg, a wholesale boot and shoe manufacturer. The Reads first occupied it in 1907. It still looks much as it did when amateur sleuths and thespians roamed its rooms.

WILLIAM CECIL READ SUMMER HOME
Relocated at 30 Peninsula Road, Dellwood, White Bear Lake
104, MAP D

One of Scott's treasured haunts during his school days was the cottage owned by Cecil Read's parents on White Bear Lake. The rambling frame structure where he spent many summer weekends had four rooms upstairs and four down, a wide and long front porch, and a sleeping porch on the side. Behind was a small barn with a hayloft where the youngsters played.[36]

After Saturday night dances at the White Bear Yacht Club, Scott and Cecil Read would slip into their beds on the screened porch, talk into the night about their futures, and let the breezes from the lake lull them to sleep. Perhaps it was during one of these late-night talks that Scott revealed to Cecil his ambition to write a great Catholic novel—an ambition he never fulfilled.

Annabel, Scott's younger sister, accompanied him at least once to the Read cottage. Too young to attend

Read summer house, White Bear Lake, 1978

the Saturday night hop, Annabel—"the essence of charming femin[in]ity"—stayed home and taught Cecil's younger brother Clifton to dance.

The cottage was sold to Francis G. Okie in 1929. The new owners moved it across the bay on the winter ice to the peninsula—a move which almost resulted in catastrophe when the ice broke and a corner of the structure began to sink. In its new location the Read cottage was added to an existing house to make a substantial summer home, which is still in use.

WORRELL CLARKSON ESTATE
94 Dellwood Avenue, Dellwood, White Bear Lake
102, MAP D

Worrell Clarkson owned one of the more exclusive estates on White Bear Lake. He also owned Clarkson Farms at nearby Withrow, and thousands of people attended the horse races at his sizable track there. Clarkson served as commodore of the White Bear Yacht Club in 1912 and was one of Dellwood's community leaders.[37]

Before the performance of Fitzgerald's play, "The Coward," at the club on September 12, 1913, the Clark-sons hosted a dinner in honor of the "young and talented actors." That fall Scott enrolled at Princeton. He maintained a friendship with Elizabeth, one of the Clarkson daughters, with whom he exchanged letters while he was a Princeton undergraduate.

The original Clarkson residence has undergone extensive remodeling, but these changes have enhanced the appearance of the structure.

Clarkson estate, White Bear Lake, 1978

ST. JOHN THE EVANGELIST EPISCOPAL CHURCH
Corner Kent Street and Portland Avenue
38, MAP A

Scott was a Princeton freshman when he went home for the Christmas holidays at the end of 1913 and committed what he considered in 1923 to be the "most disgraceful" deed of his life. On Christmas Eve, after "suppering heavily" with a friend at a house near this church, he was seized with a sudden, alcoholic yearning to sing Christmas hymns. He entered St. John's and, as St. Paul's aristocracy watched, swayed all the way down the aisle until he reached the foot of the pulpit. He looked up into the rector's face and said, "Don't mind me, go on with the sermon," then turned and walked unsteadily out of the church. His comment that the local newspapers "had the extra out before midnight" to describe his behavior appears to be, like the reports of Mark Twain's death, greatly exaggerated. St. John's Church has been enlarged since Fitzgerald's embarrassing invasion.[38]

St. John's Episcopal Church, Kent and Portland, about 1935

TOWN AND COUNTRY CLUB
2279 Marshall Avenue
49, MAP C

The Town and Country Club, located on a bluff overlooking the Mississippi River, was popular with Scott's adolescent crowd. In winter its golf course became an excellent bobsled run. Bob parties and sleighrides started at the University Club or at the home of the host or hostess and ended at Town and Country, where the young people warmed up with hot chocolate, chicken sandwiches, and dancing.[39]

Here in 1915 Fitzgerald met Ginevra King, the first serious love of his life. Ginevra was from Lake Forest, Illinois. She was rich, beautiful, poised, certain of her social position, and sought after by many young men. She was Marie Hersey's roommate at Westover, a private girls' school in the East, and her house guest over the Christmas holidays. On January 4, 1915, Elizabeth McDavitt gave a party in Ginevra's honor at the Town and Country Club, followed by supper at the McDavitt home. Scott, who was among the invited guests, promptly fell in love; for Ginevra, he was the most important of her conquests at the time.[40]

Most of their romance was carried on by letters, but there were occasional rendezvous: theater and dinner in New York City, a visit to her Lake Forest home, her visit to Princeton to attend the Yale game. They quarreled, and he was made miserable by reports of other suitors. At a party someone said, "Poor boys shouldn't think of marrying rich girls." The final break occurred in January 1917.[41]

Fitzgerald "in his schoolboy way never faltered in his devotion" to Ginevra, wrote one biographer. He kept every letter she ever wrote to him, had them typed and bound—they came to 227 pages—and until the end of his days the thought of her could bring tears to his eyes.[42]

Although he lost the real Ginevra, he put her and their affair into his fiction. The short stories, "Babes in the Woods," "The Debutante," "Basil and Cleopatra," "Winter Dreams," and, on a more cynical note, "The Pierian Spring and the Last Straw," all deal with her and with their romance. She was also the model for Isabelle in *This Side of Paradise*.[43]

The Town and Country Club, founded in 1888, was the first golf club in Minnesota. A roster of its members during the Fitzgerald era reads like a Twin Cities' Who's Who. The club is still thriving today, although the original clubhouse familiar to Fitzgerald has since been incorporated into a new and modern structure.[44]

Town and Country Club, 2279 Marshall, about 1915

THOMAS McDAVITT HOUSE
596 Grand Avenue
16, MAP A

McDavitt house, 596 Grand, 2004

The bob party at which Fitzgerald met Ginevra King in January 1915 was given by Elizabeth McDavitt, daughter of Dr. and Mrs. Thomas McDavitt. It ended with supper in the Grand Avenue home of her parents. Not only was the party a highlight of the holiday social season, chronicled in the society pages of the St. Paul newspaper, it was also an important event in Fitzgerald's life. The nineteen-year-old future novelist returned to Princeton in a rosy haze. His romance with the glamorous Ginevra was his first serious love affair, and he was heartbroken when she broke it off two years later.[45]

The McDavitt house, linked to one of the most romantic episodes in Fitzgerald's life, was rescued from demolition in the 1980s and has been renovated to hold three apartments.

F. SCOTT FITZGERALD RESIDENCE
593 Summit Avenue
83, MAP A

At the beginning of Scott's sophomore year at Princeton, in September 1914, his parents moved to one of eight attached residences in a three-story brownstone known as Summit Terrace. Although the house lacked the opulence of many other Summit Avenue homes, the Fitzgeralds for the first time were living on the street Scott would someday characterize as "a museum of American architectural failures."[46]

Scott had a third-floor retreat which he occupied for the first time when he returned from Princeton for Christmas vacation in 1914—the same holiday season he met Ginevra King. The following year he was unexpectedly back home. In December 1915—his junior year—he became ill with what was then diagnosed as malaria; it was later determined to be a light form of tuberculosis. Although the illness was real enough, it gave him a respectable opportunity to leave Princeton where he was flunking out.[47]

His eight-month recuperation in St. Paul was unhappy, aimless, and uneventful—a period of frustration and depression lightened by occasional parties and made more bleak by a case of mumps. He worried over Ginevra King getting "fired" (expelled) from Westover and the growing strain in their relationship. He paid an unhappy visit to her Lake Forest home. He tried to deal with his college failures by writing "The Spire and the Gargoyle," a story he considered to be "the beginning of mature writing." He later incorporated part of it into *This Side of Paradise*.[48]

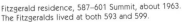

Fitzgerald residence, 587–601 Summit, about 1963.
The Fitzgeralds lived at both 593 and 599.

Fitzgerald resumed his Princeton career in the fall of 1916, but it was to be short-lived. He was barred from extracurricular activities, leaving him, he said, with "no badges of pride, no medals, after all." Ended were his hopes of being president of the Triangle, of participation in Cottage Club, of the editorship of *The Tiger,* perhaps even a seat on the senior council. It was, he wrote in his ledger, "A year of terrible disappointments & the end of all college dreams. Everything bad in it was my own fault."[49]

By the summer of 1917 the United States was at war in Europe and Scott, with some of his college and St. Paul friends, decided to volunteer. He spent one day at Fort Snelling in July taking the examinations required for appointment to officers' training school. That fall he returned to Princeton to wait. His commission came through, and in November he was ordered to report to Fort Leavenworth, Kansas.[50]

F. SCOTT FITZGERALD RESIDENCE
599 Summit Avenue
84, MAP A

This three-story apartment building near Summit and Dale—only a few doors from the house Grandmother McQuillan built—is the St. Paul address most significantly associated with F. Scott Fitzgerald. It is the residence where he completed his first novel, *This Side of Paradise.* Mollie and Edward Fitzgerald had moved there in September 1918.[51]

Since joining the army in November 1917, Fitzgerald had been working on a novel which he finished and sent to Scribner's in the spring of 1918, while he was still in camp. Maxwell Perkins, a young editor at Scribner's, sent it back with much encouragement and some detailed suggestions for revisions. Fitzgerald tried to make them and resubmitted the revised manuscript. It was again turned down—Perkins apparently having been overruled by two older editors.[52]

While he was stationed at Camp Sheridan near Montgomery, Alabama, Scott met and fell in love with Zelda Sayre. They carried on a rather nervous long-distance romance while she considered other suitors and the prospect of a life of poverty if she married Scott. In March 1919 he sent her what must have been a modest engagement ring.[53]

After Fitzgerald was discharged from the army in February 1919, he took a job as an advertising copy-writer in New York City. In June, Zelda broke off their engagement "because he had no money and could make no money." Scott went on a monumental three-week drunk, then sat down to try to sort out his life.[54]

Fitzgerald residence, 599 Summit, about 1975

This "remarkably optimistic young man," as one of his biographers characterized him, had not given up his dream of success. He quit—with relief—his job at the advertising agency, and on July 4 he left for St. Paul. He had decided to write his novel all over again, produce a best seller, and win back Zelda Sayre.[55]

Considering their attitudes, his parents were remarkably accommodating. They strongly disapproved of his writing career, which they considered a waste of time. His father wanted him to go into business; his mother wanted him to become a military man. Nevertheless they provided him with a quiet room on the third floor and respected his need for privacy during the following two months. With chapters pinned to the curtains around the room, he began systematically revising every scene that he retained and adding many new ones. He often worked around the clock. When he did not want to stop for regular meals, milk and sandwiches were brought to him. His parents kept out of the way, and his mother took telephone messages and prevented his friends from interrupting.[56]

By the end of July 1919, he had finished a new first draft. He wrote Perkins, "After four months attempt to write commercial copy by day and painful half-hearted imitations of popular literature by night I decided that it was one thing or another. So I gave up getting married and went home." He told the editor that while his earlier book had been "a tedious, disconnected casserole this is a definite attempt at a big novel and I really believe I have it." He inquired anxiously about the publication date, even though Perkins had not yet seen the revised manuscript, which had at first been entitled "The Romantic Egotist" and then "The Education of a Personage."[57]

On September 4 he mailed the new draft, now entitled "This Side of Paradise," to Perkins. While waiting for an answer, he took a job in the Northern Pacific carbarns obtained with the help of his old friend Laurence ("Larry") Boardman. Boardman had instructed Scott to report in old clothes, and Scott did, appearing for work in dirty white flannels, a polo shirt, a sweatshirt, and a blue cap. He quickly bought himself a pair of overalls, and learned not to offend the foreman by sitting down while pounding nails. After a few days, however, he quit, deciding this line of work was not for him. The wages he earned were just about wiped out when someone stole his new four-dollar pair of overalls.[58]

Fortunately, in mid-September, he received a letter from Perkins telling him Scribner's had accepted "This Side of Paradise." The elated Fitzgerald ran up and down Summit Avenue, stopping cars and telling friends and even slight acquaintances that his book had been accepted.[59]

A few days later, on September 22 (just two days before his twenty-third birthday), Fitzgerald sent off an exuberant letter to Alida Bigelow, then at Smith College, at the top of which he wrote this now-famous description of 599 Summit:

> In a house below the average
> On a street above the average
> In a room below the roof
> With a lot above the ears
> I shall write Alida Bigelow. . . .
> Scribner has accepted my book. Ain't I smart![60]

Summit Terrace was added to the National Register of Historic Places in 1972, and a plaque describing its significance was placed over the entrance. Its exterior has changed relatively little over the years. It remains a private residence not open to the public.[61]

MRS. CHARLES PORTERFIELD'S BOARDINGHOUSE
513 Summit Avenue
79, MAP A

Fitzgerald needed an occasional respite from his intense, often round-the-clock work on his first novel. In the summer of 1919 he occasionally took long walks with a relatively new acquaintance, Donald Ogden Stewart. Stewart, an aspiring young writer, and John De-Quedville Briggs, headmaster at St. Paul Academy, both lived at Mrs. Porterfield's for a time. Stewart, who later became a screenwriter, also wrote *A Parody Outline of History* as well as a spoof of Fitzgerald's work. Their walks often ended at the lodgings of Stewart and Briggs.[62]

Mrs. Porterfield's boardinghouse, 513 Summit, 1978

The comfortable Queen Anne house in which they lived was built in 1891. It boasts a pleasant front porch where, one can surmise, the three friends no doubt sat smoking and discussing literary matters.

W. A. FROST'S PHARMACY, HERMAN W. RIETZKE DRUG, GROTTO PHARMACY

374 Selby Avenue
58, MAP A
380 Selby Avenue
59, MAP A
740 Grand Avenu
20, MAP A

Two neighborhood Coke-and-smoke haunts also offered Fitzgerald escape for his labors in the summer of 1919. With Richard ("Tubby") Washington, a longtime friend who lived in the same row house on Summit, Scott would sometimes wander to the corner of Selby and Western for Cokes, cigarettes, and conversation at W. A. Frost's Pharmacy in the Dakotah Building or at Rietzke's Drug just across the street in the Angus Hotel.

W. A. Frost, 374 Selby, 1978

It was Washington who paid for the cigarettes and Cokes, since Fitzgerald's family refused to supply funds to support his writing career.[63]

Grotto Pharmacy, another nearby drugstore that was owned by Wesley ("Doc") Sinclair, was also associated with Fitzgerald. The store carried Tom Moore Cigars, which Scott's father preferred. When he returned to St. Paul as a successful novelist in 1921, Scott had an immaculate red and tan Buick touring car in which he would drive his father to the Grotto in style, much to the delight of curious Grand Avenue residents.

None of these drugstores is in business today, but two of the buildings may still be seen at the busy intersection of Selby and Western. A restaurant named for W. A. Frost does a thriving business, occupying a larger part of the Dakotah Building than did the original pharmacy. The once-elegant Angus Hotel, where Mollie Fitzgerald lived off and on after the death of Edward in 1931, has been renovated as the Blair Arcade. The building occupied by the Grotto Pharmacy has been razed.

ST. PAUL SEMINARY
2260 Summit Avenue
91, MAP C

Father Joseph Barron, one of Scott's friends in St. Paul, became dean of students at St. Paul Seminary at the youthful age of twenty-four. In 1916, during the months that Fitzgerald was in the city recuperating from "malaria," and again in 1919, while he was working on the novel that would make him famous, Scott often visited the seminary to discuss his work with Father Joe, whose own writings focused on philosophy and religion. He was frequently accompanied in 1919 by Donald Ogden Stewart, another young writer then living in St. Paul. Conversations among the three men ranged over a wide variety of subjects, religious and secular.[64]

Despite their disagreement on spiritual matters, Fitzgerald and Father Joe liked and respected each other. After what Scott called his "Last Catholic revival" in January 1918, his contact with the faith of his boyhood was limited to two formal rites—he and Zelda were married in St. Patrick's Cathedral in New York City on April 3, 1920, and their daughter was baptized at the Convent of the Visitation in 1921 with Father Joe as one of the sponsors.

At some point in their friendship, Scott and Father Joe laid out their own private golf course on the seminary grounds. Playing with only three clubs—seven and eight irons and a putter—the men zigzagged over the lawns, enjoying the exercise and the fresh air.

Father Joe remained on the staff of the St. Paul Seminary until 1926, receiving not always timely visits from Fitzgerald whenever he was in the city. The priest died in 1939.

Chapel at St. Paul Seminary, about 1900

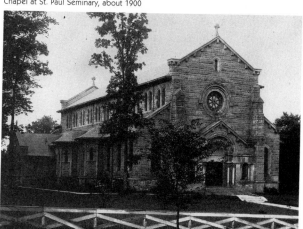

MACKEY J. THOMPSON COTTAGE
14, Highway 96, Dellwood, White Bear Lake
103, MAP D

Scott and Zelda returned to St. Paul in August 1921 to escape the hectic social life of New York and to find a quiet retreat where he could write and she could await the birth of their first child. With the help of their longtime friend Xandra Kalman, the couple rented Mackey J. Thompson's cottage located on "the Hill," an exclusive section of Dellwood on White Bear Lake. It had central heat and running water and was the only cottage in that area then equipped for year-round use. The Fitzgeralds leased it for a year, assuming that when the other residents returned to the city in September they would have the isolation they sought.[65]

It did not work out that way. An almost constant parade of old friends, new acquaintances, newspaper reporters, and well-wishers made the pilgrimage to Dellwood to see "St. Paul's first successful novelist." The young author and his wife plunged into a whirl of parties, public appearances, golf, and tennis. About all he produced in this period was one short story and a review of John Dos Passos' *Three Soldiers* for the *St. Paul Daily News.*[66]

During one of the many all-night parties at Dellwood, the furnace in the cottage went out, unnoticed by Fitzgerald, and the water pipes froze and burst. Furious about the unnecessary damage to his lovely home, Thompson asked the Fitzgeralds to leave. In early October the couple moved back to the city, staying briefly at the Hotel St. Paul and then at the Commodore Hotel.[67]

The charming New England-style cottage sits well off Highway 96 at Dellwood.

COMMODORE HOTEL
79 Western Avenue
100, MAP A

"In the fall we got to the Commodore in St. Paul, and while leaves blew up the street we waited for our child to be born," Fitzgerald wrote years later in an essay. This well-known St. Paul landmark was one of F. Scott Fitzgerald's favorite local hotels.[68]

The Fitzgeralds lived at the Commodore in 1921 and again in 1922. They enjoyed its plush comforts after being evicted from the Dellwood cottage in early October 1921, and from the Commodore Zelda went to Miller Hospital to give birth to their baby, Frances Scott ("Scottie"), on October 26, 1921. Scott wrote of the baby to Edmund Wilson, whom he had met at Princeton and who remained a lifelong friend, that "we dazzle her exquisite eyes with gold pieces in the hopes that she'll marry a millionaire." But it was Xandra Kalman who went out and bought all the clothes and other provisions needed for the baby after discovering that neither Fitzgerald had thought of anything so practical.

Commodore Hotel, 79 Western, about 1925

The Commodore once more provided a haven for the three Fitzgeralds in August 1922, after they had been ousted from the White Bear Yacht Club—or "Yatch," as Scott persisted in spelling it—and it was their final home in St. Paul.[69]

The elegant new Commodore had opened its doors in 1920 as an apartment hotel, a status it always retained. According to its advertising, the hostelry offered "a high-class Residential Service that features, among other things, the 'Home-Like Spirit,'" and a location "in the most aristocratic and quiet section of the city." Bands performed in its rooftop garden; women wore formal gowns and men black tails and white ties in its luxurious dining area. One of the hotel's striking features was its elegant Art Deco bar, which opened in the 1930s with the repeal of Prohibition. With its amber lights, mirrors, and black and white decor, it looked like something "straight out of a luxury liner."[70]

After a period of decline, the Commodore was refurbished in the 1970s. But after a major gas explosion in 1978, however, the building was subsequently developed into condominiums. The main entrance was moved from the courtyard to the north side of the building, where the explosion had opened a hole in the brickwork.[71]

FITZGERALD RESIDENCE
626 Goodrich Avenue
12, MAP A

After the birth of their daughter, the elegant transients were again rescued by Xandra Kalman, whose relatives, Mrs. Arnold (Sarah) and Cecelia Kalman, lived in this late-Victorian house. The Fitzgeralds moved in with the infant Scottie and a nurse in November 1921. At the top of an undated letter written about December 1 to his editor at Scribner's, Scott scribbled next to the Goodrich address: "New Address/Permanent!"[72]

Fitzgerald residence, 626 Goodrich, about 1976

He also rented a small, bare office in downtown St. Paul where he could work in seclusion, refusing to divulge its location except to one or two close friends. At that time Fitzgerald was working on page-proof revisions of "The Beautiful and Damned," which Scribner's would publish on April 3, 1922. He was also worrying about the jacket design for the book, Scribner's plans to promote it, and money. He wrote "The Popular Girl" and worked on a play and on a compilation of his short stories.[73]

On his daily walks from the house on Goodrich to the office, Fitzgerald often stopped at Kilmarnock Books at 84 East Fourth Street in the Guardian Building to talk and drink with proprietors Cornelius Van Ness and Thomas A. Boyd. Boyd was the literary editor of the *St. Paul Daily News* and helped keep Fitzgerald prominent on its pages. Later Scott would persuade Scribner's to publish Boyd's war novel *Through the Wheat* (1923). Among the regulars at the shop were Tom's wife Peggy, who was also a writer, and Father Joe Barron. Distinguished literary lights also dropped in to enjoy the conviviality of the bookstore's back room. There Fitzgerald met Joseph Hergesheimer, a popular author of the 1920s.[74]

With Scott gone so much, Zelda, at home with Scottie, began to get bored and depressed. She hated St. Paul, its winters, and what she regarded as its out-of-date Victorianism. The Goodrich house had been beneficial for Scott, but because of Zelda's mounting tension and restlessness, the Fitzgeralds moved in June 1922 to the White Bear Yacht Club for sunshine, relaxation, and a change of pace.[75]

This large Victorian house with a porch and cupola drew many curious people while it was the Fitzgeralds' residence, and it continues to draw occasional sight-seers. It is a private residence. Kilmarnock Books is no more. It passed to the proprietorship of Mabel Ulrich in the mid-1920s and continued to be a well-known St. Paul landmark for many years. The Guardian Building was razed in the late 1960s to make way for the Kellogg Square Apartments, which now occupies the site.[76]

UNIVERSITY CLUB
Summit Avenue and Ramsey Street
75, MAP A

While Scott and Zelda were living in St. Paul, they often visited the University Club, which had opened the doors of its new building in March 1913. Fitzgerald probably never became a member, but as a college student he had been a frequent visitor at the dances, in the dining room, and in the bar (where legend had it he carved his initials). Among his fond memories were the sleighrides and bob parties that often started at the University Club and ended at the Town and Country Club.[77]

Scott scandalized the University Club more than once. When he was nineteen or twenty, a theatrical road company visited the city and Fitzgerald sent the leading lady a note, asking if he might see her after the show. She accepted and he and a friend took her and another actress dancing. The next day the four of them shocked University Club patrons by lunching there, although it was "all perfectly innocent."[78]

Scott and Zelda loved jokes, and one of their more enduring ones was the publication of the *St. Paul Daily Dirge*, a parody of a newspaper's society page describing the University Club's "Bad Luck Ball" given on Friday, January 13, 1922. They hired a boy to peddle the paper to guests as they arrived, the price being "a sweet kiss."

University Club, Summit Ave. and Ramsey, about 1919

"Cotillion is Sad Failure," said the headline of the four-page paper, and the subhead read, "Frightful Orgy at University Club." It went on to describe the dance as "the worst failure of the year," with a "sordid fist fight" between two of St. Paul's elite, and told about other misadventures of the "vain, shallow, and frivolous society people who were present."[79]

The University Club continues in operation today. Visitors still ask to see Fitzgerald's autograph on the club's bar, but his signature is not there. The bar was signed by others during a 1936 fundraiser, long after Fitzgerald had left St. Paul.[80]

WHITE BEAR YACHT CLUB
56 Dellwood Avenue, Dellwood, White Bear Lake
101, MAP D

From the time he was thirteen until he left St. Paul for good at the age of twenty-six, Scott Fitzgerald was a regular visitor at the White Bear Yacht Club, which could be easily reached via interurban electric streetcar from St. Paul. With Cecil Read, Robert Clark, Gustave B. ("Bobbie") Schurmeier, Reuben Warner, and George Squires, he swam, sailed, played tennis, and hiked—along with less clublike pursuits such as skinning gophers and stealing candy.[81]

Of more importance to his later literary career were his theatrical activities. A Civil War drama, "The Coward," which he wrote for the Elizabethan Dramatic Club, was staged in late August 1913, first at the Young Women's Christian Association in St. Paul and a week later at the White Bear Yacht Club. For all practical purposes Scott was producer and director as well as author and actor. During the performance at the club, a youth playing a role which required him to handle a pistol discovered a live bullet in the prop weapon and precipitously left the stage to run out and discharge it at the end of the dock. The quick-witted Fitzgerald filled the otherwise-awkward interim with some hastily invented dialogue.[82]

The next year Scott wrote for Magoffin a farce called "Assorted Spirits," which was also produced a second time at the club, largely under his direction. Once more his resourcefulness saved the day when the lights suddenly went out during a ghost scene. To calm the panicky audience Scott jumped on the stage and delivered an improvised monologue while the electrician repaired the lighting problem.[83]

The White Bear Yacht Club was also the scene of many summer Saturday night dances, which Scott often attended. The beautiful lake, the moonlight, the music, and the rich and pretty girls created an atmosphere that is partly reflected in his short story, "Winter Dreams." (Ginevra King, his first real love, is the Judy Jones of that story.) Written in the summer of 1922 just after Fitzgerald and his wife moved from the White Bear Yacht Club where they had been living, the story is one of the few things that Scott completed during those unproductive months.[84]

White Bear Yacht Club, about 1915

In June 1922, to combat Zelda's unhappiness in St. Paul, she, Scott, and nine-month-old Scottie had moved to the club for a change of scene. Feeling that he was temporarily in a slump, Scott tried to work on a collection of short stories and intermittently on a play. He wrote Maxwell Perkins at Scribner's that the play was the best thing he had ever done, that it would make him so rich and famous he would never have to bother Perkins about money again—he had just requested a $1,000 loan against future royalties from *The Beautiful and Damned,* which had been published in April. He toyed with an idea for a novel and horrified Perkins by considering a proposal that he and Zelda play the leading roles in a motion picture based on *This Side of Paradise.*[85]

Sinclair Lewis visited the Fitzgeralds that summer—the most notable of a steady stream of visitors. The club was conveniently at the center of the summer parties, and the tempo and intensity of partying always increased in the vicinity of Scott and Zelda. Both of them believed that "if you were good enough you not only could live according to the hedonistic code of the twenties but would probably turn out better for doing so."[86]

White Bear Yacht Club officials did not, however, share this view, and at the end of August they asked the Fitzgeralds to leave. Neither raised any objections—they longed to return to New York—and like abdicating royalty they packed up and departed from Dellwood and from Minnesota forever.[87]

Although the original clubhouse was destroyed by fire in 1937, another was constructed near the site and is still in operation.

MAPS

These maps indicated the locations of the buildings listed on pages 61–80. The buildings that Fitzgerald lived in or frequented, featured on pages 13–56, are marked on the maps as indicated below and highlighted in the list on pages 61–80 with an asterisk. The number treatment on the map also shows whether the building still stands.

KEY

16 Building is featured on preceding pages and still stands

19 Building is featured on preceding pages but has been razed

17 Building still stands

⟨*18*⟩ Building has been razed

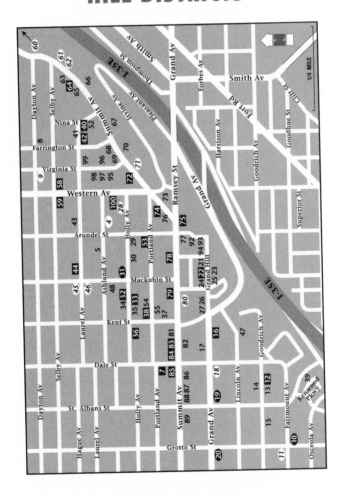

MAP B
DOWNTOWN ST. PAUL

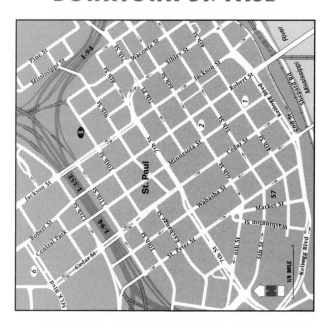

MAP C
ST. PAUL'S WEST END

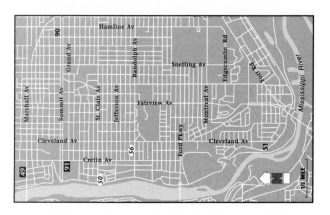

MAP D
WHITE BEAR LAKE/DELLWOOD

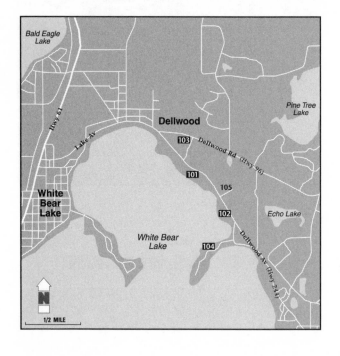

FITZGERALD BUILDINGS IN ST. PAUL

The list below, organized alphabetically by street, includes the houses, schools, churches, clubs, and other buildings in St. Paul and White Bear Lake that are known to have connections to F. Scott Fitzgerald. The sites that have been more fully described in the preceding pages are marked with asterisks and included here to facilitate walking tours. Most of the buildings are still standing; those that have been razed are so indicated. The terms "house" and "residence" are used to differentiate between those places which were more or less permanent, fixed abodes (usually owned by the person or the parents of the person who was significant in Fitzgerald's life) and those which were temporary residences, apartment houses, boardinghouses, or other less permanent dwellings.

1. 84 EAST FOURTH ST. Kilmarnock Books. This bookstore was a meeting place for local and visiting literary lights, and FSF was a frequent visitor. Razed.

2. SIXTH ST. BETWEEN ROBERT AND MINNESOTA STREETS. Metropolitan Opera House. Legitimate theater productions were given here and in later years it was also used as a movie house. Scott and his friends probably attended both plays and movies here. Razed.

*3. 249 EAST TENTH ST. Philip F. and Louisa A. McQuillan house in Lowertown. Razed. (See page 13.)

4. 404 ASHLAND AVE. George E. Ingersoll house. Daughter Jean was a friend of FSF; her mother, Janey McLaren Ingersoll, organized the dancing class. Razed.

Metropolitan Opera House, Sixth St. between Robert and Minnesota, about 1919

5. 457 ASHLAND AVE. Cecil Read house. Cecil was a close friend of FSF. (See also nos. 53 and 77.)

6. 77 EAST CENTRAL AVE. Mrs. Gustave F. (Rose) Schurmeier house. Son Gustave B. ("Bobbie") was a good friend of FSF. Razed. (See also no. 86.)

*7. 25 NORTH DALE ST. St. Paul Academy. FSF attended the prep school for three years. (See page 20.)

8. 314 DAYTON AVE. Ambrose Tighe house. Daughter Katherine was a good friend of FSF, especially in the later St. Paul years.

9. 350 DAYTON AVE. Aberdeen Hotel. Mollie Fitzgerald stayed here briefly after the family returned to St. Paul. Razed.

Tighe house, 314 Dayton, 1941

Aberdeen Hotel, 350 Dayton, about 1900

*10. 720 FAIRMOUNT AVE.   Convent of the Visitation. Mollie Fitzgerald's alma mater; Scottie Fitzgerald was baptized here. Razed. (See page 19.)

11. 745 FAIRMOUNT AVE.   John Fulton house. (See also no. 63.) Razed.

*12. 626 GOODRICH AVE.   FSF residence. (See page 50.)

13. 642 GOODRICH AVE.   Henry J. Horn house. Daughter Margaret was a friend of FSF and a member of the dancing class.

14. 653 GOODRICH AVE.   Forrest Orton house. Daughter Joanne was a friend of FSF and a dancing class colleague. On at least one occasion he went to a sleighride party she hosted.

15. 708 GOODRICH AVE.   Walter E. Alair house. Daughter Eleanor was a good friend of FSF; it was she whom the children in Professor Baker's class tried to petition into dancing school.

Horn House, 642 Goodrich, about 1973

*16. 596 GRAND AVE. Thomas McDavitt house. Daughter Elizabeth, a member of the Elizabethan Dramatic Club, gave the party at which FSF met Ginevra King. (See page 39.)

17. 614 GRAND AVE. Worrell Clarkson house. Daughter Elizabeth was a good friend of FSF. (See also no. 102.)

18. 654 GRAND AVE. Edward P. James house. Daughter Constance was a good friend of FSF. Razed.

*19. 664–668 GRAND AVE. Ramaley Hall, where Professor Baker's dancing class was held. Razed. (See page 26.)

*20. 740 GRAND AVE. Grotto Pharmacy, where Edward Fitzgerald bought his cigars. Razed. (See page 45.)

21. 483 GRAND HILL. John N. Jackson house. Son Norris was a good friend of FSF.†

*22. 501 GRAND HILL. Charles W. Ames house. Son Theodore ("Ted") and daughter Elizabeth were friends of FSF; Ames's yard was a setting for "The Scandal Detectives." (See page 28.)

23. 506 GRAND HILL. James D. Armstrong house. Daughter Margaret was a close friend of FSF and probably the Imogene Bissel of "The Scandal Detectives."

24. 511 GRAND HILL. Silas M. Ford house. Daughter Ardietta was a good friend of FSF. (See also no. 71.)

---

† At the behest of the Grand Avenue Businessmen's Association, which wanted a Grand Avenue entrance and exit from Interstate 35E, Oakland Avenue was renamed Grand Avenue, except for one block between Summit and Grand which remains Oakland. The two-block stretch of the former Grand Avenue between Oakland and Summit Court is now named Grand Hill.

Armstrong house, 506 Grand Hill, 1978

25. 514 GRAND HILL. William J. Dean house. Daughter Elisabeth was a good friend and confidante of FSF. (See also no. 74.)

26. 549 GRAND HILL. Edward and Mollie Fitzgerald residence.

27. 561 GRAND HILL. Mrs. William R. (Helen T.) Dorr house. Daughter Julia was a good friend of FSF. She once organized an expedition to a haunted house on Pleasant Ave. Scott "lost" Margaret Armstrong to James Porterfield en route.

28. 413 HOLLY AVE. Austin Ballion house. Son Paul was one of FSF's close boyhood friends and the Bill Kempf of the Basil Duke Lee stories. Razed.

29. 454 HOLLY AVE. Charles A. Clark house. Son Robert D. and daughter Caroline were both friends of FSF; Bob was part of a close circle. (See also no. 96.)

Fitzgerald residence, 549 Grand Hill, 1978

Ballion house, 413 Holly, about 1973

30. 472 HOLLY AVE. Mrs. Philip F. (Louisa A.) McQuillan residence.

*31. 499 HOLLY AVE. FSF residence. Razed. (See page 24.)

*32. 509 HOLLY AVE. FSF residence. (See page 24.)

*33. 514 HOLLY AVE. FSF residence. (See page 24.)

34. 529 HOLLY AVE. Paul C. Weed house. Daughter Emily Lucile, a friend of FSF's sister, later became Mrs. Cecil Read.

35. 546 HOLLY AVE. Dr. Benjamin H. Ogden house. Ogden was the physician who delivered FSF.

*36. 580–590 HOLLY AVE. Mrs. Backus' School for Girls. Many of FSF's female friends attended the school; he took Margaret Armstrong to a dance there, and one of FSF's theatrical productions was staged in Oak Hall. (See page 27.)

37. 20 NORTH KENT ST. Mrs. Maude Winchester house. Daughter Margaret was a good friend of FSF.

*38. KENT ST. AND PORTLAND AVE. St. John the Evangelist Episcopal Church. FSF made an embarrassing, drunken Christmas Eve visit to this church. (See page 36.)

39. 26 KENWOOD PARKWAY. Philip McQuillan residence. He was an uncle of FSF.

*40. 286 LAUREL AVE. (Laurel Terrace or Riley Row.) Mrs. Philip F. (Louisa A.) McQuillan residence. (See page 17.)

41. 292 LAUREL AVE. Daniel Mudge house. Betty, Archie, and Dudley Mudge were friends of FSF.

McQuillan residence, 26 Kenwood Parkway, 1976

*42. 294 LAUREL AVE. FSF residence; Louisa McQuillan also lived here. (See page 17.)

43. 415 LAUREL AVE. Charles Bigelow house. Alida and Donald were close friends of FSF and members of the dancing class. To Alida FSF wrote his famous description of 599 Summit Ave.

*44. 481 LAUREL AVE. FSF birthplace. (See page 14.)

45. 497–499 LAUREL AVE. William H. Kane Grocery. FSF's first outings as an infant were to this establishment and the one across the street. Razed.

46. 500 LAUREL AVE. John Lambert's Notions. FSF's first outings as an infant were to this establishment and the one across the street. Razed.

47. 598 LINCOLN AVE. Laurence Boardman house. (See also no. 51.)

48. 79 MACKUBIN ST. Edward and Mollie Fitzgerald lived here from 1893 to 1895 or 1896, then briefly at 548 Portland, before moving to 481 Laurel where Scott was born.

*49. 2279 MARSHALL AVE. Town and Country Club. FSF met Ginevra King here. (See page 37.)

50. MISSISSIPPI RIVER BLVD. AND ST. CLAIR AVE. Cornelius Van Ness house. Co-owner of Kilmarnock Books. Razed.

51. 1590 MISSISSIPPI RIVER BLVD. Mrs. Henry A. (Cornelia) Boardman house. Laurence Boardman was a good friend of FSF and a member of the Elizabethan Dramatic Club. He helped FSF get a job at the Northern Pacific carbarns.

52. 123 NINA AVE. Mrs. William Cecil (Laura) Read house. Son Cecil was one of FSF's closest friends. (See also no. 53.) Samuel D. Sturgis, another friend, also lived in this row house for a time. (See also no. 93.)

*53. 449 PORTLAND AVE. William Cecil Read house. Son Cecil was a close friend of FSF and the Ripley Buckner of the Basil Duke Lee stories. The Read attic was a setting in "The Scandal Detectives" and the scene of some youthful FSF theatrical productions. (See page 33; see also nos. 5, 52, and 77.)

54. 523 PORTLAND AVE. Lucius P. Ordway, Jr., and John Ordway house. The Ordways were friends of FSF.

55. 548 PORTLAND AVE. Edward and Mollie Fitzgerald residence.

56. 2115 RANDOLPH AVE. Thomas A. Boyd residence. Razed. (See also no. 60.)

57. 363 ST. PETER ST. Hotel St. Paul. Scott and Zelda briefly stayed here.

*58. 374 SELBY AVE. W. A. Frost's Pharmacy. An occasional haunt of FSF when he was revising *This Side of Paradise*. (See page 45.)

*59. 380 SELBY AVE. Herman W. F. Rietzke Drug (Angus Hotel, Blair House). An occasional haunt of FSF when he was revising *This Side of Paradise*. (See page 45.)

60. 147 SUMMIT AVE. Thomas A. Boyd residence. He and wife Margaret ("Peggy"), also a novelist, were

St. Paul Hotel, 363 St. Peter, 1933

Rietzke Drug and Angus Hotel, 380 Selby (now Blair House), about 1920

friends of FSF. Boyd was co-owner of Kilmarnock Books, literary editor of the *St. Paul Daily News,* and author of *Through the Wheat* (1923). Razed. (See also no. 56.)

61. 226 SUMMIT AVE. Theodore A. Schulze house. Daughter Katharine was a friend of FSF and a member of the Elizabethan Dramatic Club. Razed.

62. 236 SUMMIT AVE. Mrs. Thomas (Jessie) Foley residence. Son Arthur C. was a childhood friend of FSF. Razed.

63. 239 SUMMIT AVE. John A. Fulton residence. Fulton, a physician, was a friend of Edward and Mollie Fitzgerald, and they stayed with him briefly after returning to St. Paul. (See also no. 11.)

*64. 245 SUMMIT AVE. George R. Finch house. Violet Stockton visited Mrs. Finch, her aunt, in 1908 and had a youthful summer romance with FSF. (See page 22.)

65. 251 SUMMIT AVE. John R. Mitchell house. Son John ("Jack") and daughter Eleanor were friends of FSF. (See also no. 70.)

66. 260 SUMMIT AVE. Louis Hill house (Maryhill). Hill, son of railroad magnate James J. Hill, held parties and dances which FSF sometimes attended.

67. 312 SUMMIT AVE. Arthur B. Driscoll house. Sons Donald and Egbert were friends of FSF. This is the oldest house standing on Summit.

68. 335 SUMMIT AVE. Sidney R. Stronge house. He was a friend of FSF. (See also no. 97.)

Driscoll house, 312 Summit, 1978

69. 339 SUMMIT AVE. Charles H. F. Smith house. Son Wharton C. and FSF bicycled to Hastings and back during one summer.

70. 340 SUMMIT AVE. John R. Mitchell house. Son John ("Jack") and daughter Eleanor were friends of FSF. (See also no. 65.)

71. 354 SUMMIT AVE. Silas M. Ford house. Daughter Ardietta was a childhood friend of FSF. Razed. (See also no. 24.)

*72. 365 SUMMIT AVE. C. Milton Griggs house. Benjamin G. Griggs was a friend and a classmate of FSF at St. Paul Academy and a member of the dancing class. (See page 32.)

73. 400 SUMMIT AVE. Lucius P. Ordway, Sr., house. Daughter Katherine was a friend of FSF. (See also no. 89.)

*74. 415 SUMMIT AVE. William J. Dean house. Daughter Elisabeth was a close friend and confidante of FSF. (See page 30; see also no. 25.)

*75. 420 SUMMIT AVE. University Club. Scene of numerous dances and other festivities; Scott and Zelda published the *St. Paul Daily Dirge* for the club's "Bad Luck Ball" in 1922. (See page 52.)

76. 421 SUMMIT AVE. Charles L. Greene house. Daughter Dorothy was a friend of FSF and a member of the Elizabethan Dramatic Club.

77. 442 SUMMIT AVE. (Summit Court apartments.) Mrs. Charles (Katherine K. T.) Porterfield residence; Mrs. William Cecil (Laura) Read residence. James Porterfield and Cecil Read, two of FSF's closest friends, both lived in this apartment building for a time. (See also nos. 5, 53, and 79.)

Summit Court Apartments, 442 Summit, 1944

*78. 475 SUMMIT AVE. Edward L. Hersey house. Daughter Marie was one of FSF's closest friends during his boyhood and later when he became a successful young writer. She was probably Margaret Torrence in "The Scandal Detectives." (See page 29.)

*79. 513 SUMMIT AVE. Mrs. Porterfield's boardinghouse. John DeQuedville Briggs and Donald Ogden Stewart, friends of FSF, both briefly resided at this lodginghouse. Briggs was headmaster of St. Paul Academy. Stewart was another aspiring young writer who worked as a clerk for the telephone company while he lived in St. Paul, about the time FSF was completing *This Side of Paradise*. (See page 44; see also no. 53.)

80. 540 SUMMIT AVE. Samuel M. Magoffin house. Daughter Elizabeth organized the Elizabethan Dramatic Club. Razed.

81. 587 SUMMIT AVE. Richard ("Tubby") Washington residence. Washington, a friend since childhood, lived in the same row house when FSF was finishing *This Side of Paradise*.

82. 590 SUMMIT AVE. Mr. and Mrs. Charles O. (Alexandra) Kalman house. Xandra Kalman, especially, was a close friend and a frequent rescuer of Scott, Zelda, and Scottie. (See also no. 105.)

*83. 593 SUMMIT AVE. FSF residence. (See page 39.)

*84. 599 SUMMIT AVE. FSF residence. (See page 41.)

*85. 623 SUMMIT AVE. Mrs. Philip F. (Louisa A.) McQuillan house. FSF's grandmother had this house built for herself, but lived here less than three years. (See page 16.)

86. 644 SUMMIT AVE. Mrs. Gustave F. (Rose) Schurmeier house. Son Gustave B. ("Bobbie") was a close friend of FSF and a member of the Elizabethan Dramatic Club. (See also no. 6.)

Kalman house, 590 Summit, 1978

87. 672 SUMMIT AVE. Allen and Annabel McQuillan residence. They were a brother and a sister of FSF's mother.

88. 676 SUMMIT AVE. Allen McQuillan residence.

89. 700 SUMMIT AVE. Lucius P. Ordway, Jr., house. The Ordways were friends of FSF. (See also no. 73.)

90. 1347 SUMMIT AVE. Pierce Butler house. FSF stayed at the Butler summer cottage at Frontenac in 1908.

*91. 2260 SUMMIT AVE. St. Paul Seminary. Father Joseph Barron, dean of the school, became a close friend and confidant of the young novelist. (See page 46.)

92. 11 SUMMIT COURT. Allen McQuillan residence.

93. 27 SUMMIT COURT. Samuel D. Sturgis residence. FSF and Sturgis often went to matinees at the Orpheum Theatre together. (See also no. 52.)

Sturgis residence, 27 Summit Court, 1978

94. 33 SUMMIT COURT. Reuben Warner house. Reuben was a friend and rival of FSF and the Hubert Blair of the Basil Duke Lee stories.

Warner house, 33 Summit Court, 1978

95. 89 VIRGINIA ST. Charles P. Noyes house. Son Larry was an acquaintance of FSF, but the latter apparently got drunk at the Noyes's house and the two had a falling-out.

96. 96 VIRGINIA ST. Charles A. Clark house. Son Robert D. and daughter Caroline were close friends of FSF. (See also no. 29.)

97. 107 VIRGINIA ST. Sidney R. Stronge house. He was one of FSF's close friends. (See also no. 68.)

98. 121 VIRGINIA ST. McNeil V. Seymour house. "Mac" was a close friend of FSF and a fellow member of the dancing class.

Noyes house, 89 Virginia, about 1965

99. 130 VIRGINIA ST. John Townsend house. Son Theodore ("Ted") and daughter Julia were good friends of FSF.

*100. 79 WESTERN AVE. Commodore Hotel. Scott and Zelda stayed here twice for brief periods. (See page 49.)

WHITE BEAR LAKE

*101. 56 DELLWOOD AVE. White Bear Yacht Club. FSF was a frequent visitor here from boyhood on, and he and Zelda lived here for a time. The clubhouse in which they lived burned in 1937; a new one was built the next year. (See page 54.)

*102. 94 DELLWOOD AVE. Worrell Clarkson summer home. Daughter Elizabeth and FSF were good friends. (See page 35; see also no. 17.)

*103. 14, HIGHWAY 96, DELLWOOD. Mackey J. Thompson home. FSF and Zelda lived here. (See page 48.)

*104. 30 PENINSULA ROAD, DELLWOOD. William Cecil Read summer home. Cecil Read was a close friend of FSF. The house has been relocated. (See page 34; see also no. 53.)

105. 5 YELLOW BIRCH ROAD, DELLWOOD. Charles O. and Xandra Kalman summer home. The Kalmans were good friends of Scott and Zelda. (See also no. 82.)

OLD FRONTENAC

106. LAKE SIDE HOTEL AND RESORT. On Lake Pepin. Located 1½ miles northeast of U.S. Highway 61 on Goodhue County Road 2 (not on maps). FSF spent ten days in July 1909 with the Pierce Butler family in a cottage adjoining the fashionable three-story hotel, which attracted Twin Cities society as well as wealthy people from other parts of the nation. The hotel and cottages have been used as a church camp, a resort, and individual vacation homes. They are now being renovated.

Lake Side Hotel and cottages at the Frontenac Resort
on the shores of Lake Pepin, about 1920

NOTES

INTRODUCTION, PAGES 3–12

1. Matthew Bruccoli, *Some Sort of Epic Grandeur,* 408–10 (2d rev. ed. Columbia, S.C., 2002).

2. On White Bear Lake, see Fitzgerald, "The Rich Boy," in Malcolm Cowley, ed. *The Stories of F. Scott Fitzgerald,* 177 (New York, 1951); Arthur Mizener, *The Far Side of Paradise: A Biography of F. Scott Fitzgerald,* 13 (Boston, 1949).

3. Scott's aunt, Mrs. Philip L. (Lorena) McQuillan, had a summer cottage at Bald Eagle Lake. See F. Scott Fitzgerald, *Ledger,* 164 (Washington, D.C., 1972). This is a published facsimile of a handwritten ledger Fitzgerald began keeping in 1919 or 1920. The original belongs to Fitzgerald scholar Matthew J. Bruccoli. It is an adult, professional record, written in the third person singular, and it is divided into five sections: "Record of published Fiction—Novels, Plays, Stories"; "Money Earned by Writing since Leaving Army"; "Published Miscelani (including movies) for which I was Paid" (his poor spelling was legendary); "Zelda's Earnings"; and "Outline Chart of my Life." In the introduction to the *Ledger,* Bruccoli says that "it is the most useful bio-bibliographical document for Fitzgerald, and I know of nothing like it for any other American author."

4. Fitzgerald, *Ledger,* 163; Minnesota Department of Natural Resources, *Frontenac State Park* (Spring, 1978), brochure and map; Jean Ingersoll Summersby to the author, November 12, 1976. Mrs. Summersby wrote that "The toboggan slide in our yard [*404 Ashland*] was built to my father's specifications. He used to go out on the coldest nights and pour pails of water down the slide to give us a faster run. We could then coast to the far side of Western Avenue.

"Our yard was the center of activity during the winter months. The gang collected there. Among those who came were Alida and Donald Bigelow, Bob and Carrie Clark, the

Driscoll twins, Cecil Read, Phillip Stringer, Arthur Foley as well as Scott Fitzgerald.

"One of our haunts was the candy store of George J. Smith on East 6th Street near Robert Street. There we used to congregate. A feature of Smith's was that each table was equipped with a telephone by which one could place an order for ice cream, etc."

The second Pierce Butler was U.S. Supreme Court justice from 1922 until his death in 1939. The elegant, old resort community has faded. Frontenac State Park now surrounds but does not include Old Frontenac.

5. Fitzgerald, *Ledger,* 163.

6. Fitzgerald, *Ledger,* 170.

7. Mizener, *Far Side of Paradise,* 1–3, 8, 11; Andrew Turnbull, *Scott Fitzgerald,* 6 (New York, 1962).

8. Turnbull, *Fitzgerald,* 7, 16, 18; Fitzgerald, *Ledger,* 152, 155, 158, 165.

9. Fitzgerald, *Ledger,* 152–158, 164; Mizener, *Far Side of Paradise,* 12; *Thoughtbook of Francis Scott Key Fitzgerald,* xxi, xxix (Princeton, N.J., 1965). These are the surviving pages of an adolescent diary Scott kept. The entries extend from August 1910 to February 1911. The original diary is owned by Mrs. C. Grove ("Scottie") Smith, the Fitzgeralds' daughter.

10. Turnbull, *Fitzgerald,* 22; Fitzgerald, *Ledger,* 164, 165, 172, 174.

11. Cowley, quoted in Mizener, *Far Side of Paradise,* 60.

12. Mizener, *Far Side of Paradise,* 83; Fitzgerald, "My Lost City," in Edmund Wilson, ed., *The Crack-Up, With other Uncollected Pieces, Note-Books and Unpublished Letters,* 29 (New York, [1945]). Fitzgerald wrote about New York City, not St. Paul, in this essay.

13. Hersey, quoted in Matthew J. Bruccoli, Scottie Fitzgerald Smith, and Joan P. Kerr, eds., *The Romantic Egoists,* 25 (New York, 1974). This "pictorial autobiography" was named for the first title Fitzgerald gave to his first book, which eventually became *This Side of Paradise.* The editors altered the spelling from Fitzgerald's "The Romantic Egotist."

14. The stories cited here appear in John Kuehl and Jackson R. Bryer, eds., *The Basil and Josephine Stories* (New York, 1973), and Cowley, ed., *Stories of Fitzgerald.*

15. Fitzgerald, *The Great Gatsby,* 176 (Reprint ed., New York, [1945]).

16. Patricia Kane, "F. Scott Fitzgerald's St. Paul: A Writer's Use of Material," in *Minnesota History,* 45:141 (Winter, 1976).

17. Ernest R. Sandeen, *St. Paul's Historic Summit Avenue,* 1 (St. Paul, 1978).

FITZGERALD'S LIFE IN ST. PAUL, PAGES 13–56

1. C[hristopher] C. Andrews, ed., *History of St. Paul, Minn.,* 174, 433 (Syracuse, N.Y., 1890); *St. Paul Pioneer Press,* April 13, 14, 1877; *St. Paul Dispatch,* April 11, 13, 17, 1877; St. Paul city directories, 1871–73.

2. Turnbull, *Fitzgerald,* 3, 4; undated newspaper clipping owned by author; *Grand Gazette,* April 19, 1976, p. 2, 3.

3. Turnbull, *Fitzgerald,* 3, 4; *St. Paul Pioneer Press,* April 14, 1877; *Grand Gazette,* April 19, 1976, p. 2, 3; Henry A. Castle, *History of St. Paul and Vicinity,* 1:345 (Chicago, 1912).

4. Mizener, *Far Side of Paradise,* 1; birth certificate of Francis Scott Key Fitzgerald, Division of Public Health, St. Paul, copy owned by author; Sue E. Holbert and June D. Holmquist, *A History Tour of 50 Twin City Landmarks,* 14 (St. Paul, 1966).

5. Baptismal certificate of F. Scott Fitzgerald, Cathedral of St. Paul, October 6, 1896, copy owned by author; Turnbull, *Fitzgerald,* 7; St. Paul city directory, 1896; Fitzgerald, *Ledger,* 151.

6. Mizener, *Far Side of Paradise,* 1; Fitzgerald, *Ledger,* 152.

7. Turnbull, *Fitzgerald,* 6; Mizener, *Far Side of Paradise,* 9, 12; Henry Dan Piper, *F. Scott Fitzgerald: A Critical Portrait,* 7 (Chicago, 1965); Fitzgerald, *Ledger,* 152–158; Sandeen, *Historic Summit Avenue,* 91.

8. For the information here and below, see *Grand Gazette,* April 19, 1976, p. 2, 3; Sandeen, *Historic Summit Avenue,* 100; Mizener, *Far Side of Paradise,* 9; Fitzgerald, *Ledger,* 153.

9. Mizener, *Far Side of Paradise,* 12–15; Fitzgerald, *Ledger,* 162; *Grand Gazette,* April 19, 1976, p. 2, 3; St. Paul city directory, 1908; Turnbull, *Fitzgerald,* 18.

10. Mizener, *Far Side of Paradise,* 2, 7, 14, 15.

11. Fitzgerald, *Ledger,* 163, 164.

12. H. F. Koeper and Eugene D. Becker, *Historic St. Paul Buildings,* 71 (St. Paul, 1964).

13. Turnbull, *Fitzgerald,* 6, 7, 22; Fitzgerald, *Ledger,* 163.

14. For the information here and below, see *Vision* (Convent of the Visitation newspaper), Spring, 1978 [p. 42], copy in MHS; *Minneapolis Tribune,* October 27, 1964, p. 15, 16; Sister Mary Regina McCabe, Mother Superior of Visitation Convent, to author (response to author written on his undated letter).

15. Mizener, *Far Side of Paradise,* 16; Fitzgerald, *Ledger,* 163.

16. For information here and below, see Turnbull, *Fitzger-*

ald, 20–22; Fitzgerald, *Ledger,* 162, 163, 165; Mizener, *Far Side of Paradise,* 16, 31, 40.

17. Mizener, *Far Side of Paradise,* 18; *Now and Then* (St. Paul Academy magazine), September 1909, p. 4–8, copy in MHS.

18. For information here and below, see Mizener, *Far Side of Paradise,* 19, 20.

19. John S. Fitch, *Some Aspects of SPA and SPA/SS in Recognition of the Seventy-Fifth Anniversary Year,* 1, 25 (St. Paul, 1976); interview with Jack Young, Amherst Wilder Foundation, July 21, 1978.

20. For the information here and below, see Turnbull, *Fitzgerald,* 24; Fitzgerald, *Ledger,* 152; Sandeen, *Historic Summit Avenue,* 50; Fitzgerald, *Thoughtbook,* viii–xvii.

21. Mizener, *Far Side of Paradise,* 13; Fitzgerald, *Ledger,* 164.

22. Fitzgerald, *Ledger,* 165, 166; *St. Paul Dispatch,* May 23, 1910, p. 1, 2; June 10, 1910, p. 18; Lucy Fricke, *Historic Ramsey Hill: Yesterday, Today, Tomorrow* [p. 4] (St. Paul, [197?]).

23. Mizener, *Far Side of Paradise,* 13, 19. Turnbull, in his biography of Fitzgerald (338, note 31), says that Scott's sister Annabel told him that Aunt Annabel McQuillan did not pay Scott's way at Newman, but she did offer to pay his way if he would go to Catholic Georgetown University, which Edward Fitzgerald had attended.

24. Fitzgerald, *Ledger,* 166; Mizener, *Far Side of Paradise,* 20.

25. Sandeen, *Historic Summit Avenue,* 92.

26. On the dancing class here and below, see Fitzgerald, *Thoughtbook,* xxix, xxx; Summersby to author, November 12, 1976; Clifton Read to author, May 17, 1976; Turnbull, *Fitzgerald,* 22; University Club of St. Paul, "F. Scott Fitzgerald Follies," program, 1973, p. 14. The photograph on page 14 of the program is identified in Bruccoli, Smith, and Kerr, eds., *Romantic Egoists,* 13, as a picture of a St. Paul Academy pageant, but the club program and Jean Summersby's letter both indicate it is of the dancing class.

27. St. Paul city directories, 1908–16. For the information below, see Fitzgerald, *Thoughtbook,* xxxv; Fitzgerald, *Ledger,* 165; Mizener, *Far Side of Paradise,* 25.

28. *St. Paul Dispatch,* March 7, 1962, p. 26; Fitzgerald, *Ledger,* 165; "The Scandal Detectives," in Cowley, ed., *Stories of Fitzgerald,* 309–326; *Minneapolis Star,* October 27, 1964, p. 15. On Charles Ames, see Warren Upham and Rose B. Dunlap, *Minnesota Biographies, 1655–1912,* 11 (*Minnesota Historical Collections,* vol. 14, 1912).

29. Fitzgerald, *Thoughtbook,* xx, xxi, xxix; Fitzgerald, *Ledger,*

162, 165; Turnbull, *Fitzgerald*, 30; Upham and Dunlap, *Minnesota Biographies*, 322.

30. Here and below, see Bruccoli, Smith, and Kerr, eds., *Romantic Egoists*, 25, 26; Fitzgerald, *Ledger*, 170, 171; Turnbull, *Fitzgerald*, 54; Sandeen, *Historic Summit Avenue*, 70.

31. On the Deans, see Upham and Dunlap, *Minnesota Biographies*, 170; Fitzgerald, *Thoughtbook*, xxv–xxxx; Fitzgerald, *Ledger*, 165; Mrs. Walter Kennedy (Elisabeth Dean), to author, December, 1976; Fitzgerald, "The Scandal Detectives," in Cowley, ed., *Stories of Fitzgerald*, 309–325.

32. Sandeen, *Historic Summit Avenue*, 66; St. Paul city directories, 1906–08.

33. C. Milton Griggs reportedly offered Fitzgerald a job at an "impressive" salary as advertising manager at Griggs Cooper and Company. Although Scribner's had not yet accepted *This Side of Paradise*, Fitzgerald was apparently so confident of his ultimate success as a novelist—and perhaps equally sure that he would never be happy writing "commercial copy"—that he turned Griggs down, much to the dismay of his parents. On the Griggs family and house here and below, see Mizener, *Far Side of Paradise*, 86; Upham and Dunlap, *Minnesota Biographies*, 279; Fitzgerald, *Thoughtbook*, xxix, xxxix; Benjamin Griggs to author, April 13, 1976; Sandeen, *Historic Summit Avenue*, 64.

34. Mizener, *Far Side of Paradise*, 16, 17, 318n; Fitzgerald, *Thoughtbook*, xx, xxi, xxix, xxx, xxxiii; Fitzgerald, *Ledger*, 164, 165; Fitzgerald, "The Scandal Detectives," in Cowley, ed., *Stories of Fitzgerald*, 307–325.

35. For information here and below see Mrs. Herbert Lewis (Emily Lucile Weed), formerly Mrs. Cecil Read, to author, January 1, 1977; Clifton Read to author, December 3, 1976; Fricke, *Historic Ramsey Hill*, [p. 3]; St. Paul city directories, 1883–1914.

36. Information on the Read summer home is based on Clifton Read to author, January 8, 1977 (quoted two paragraphs below); Mrs. Lewis to author, January 1, 1977; Fitzgerald, *Ledger*, 164, 165.

37. Carl B. Drake *et al.*, *White Bear Yacht Club: Its History*, 141 (St. Paul, 1961); Bruccoli, Smith, and Kerr, eds., *Romantic Egoists*, 18; Fitzgerald, *Ledger*, 167.

38. Mizener, *Far Side of Paradise*, 27; Fitzgerald, "The Most Disgraceful Thing I Ever Did," in Matthew J. Bruccoli and Jackson R. Bryer, eds., *In His Own Time: A Miscellany*, 234 (Kent, Ohio, 1971). A search of St. Paul newspapers disclosed no such account.

39. Summersby to author, November 20, 1976; Fitzgerald, *Ledger*, 165, 176; Turnbull, *Fitzgerald*, 23.

40. Mizener, *Far Side of Paradise*, 47; Bruccoli, Smith, and Kerr, eds., *Romantic Egoists*, 26; Fitzgerald, *Ledger*, 169.

41. Mizener, *Far Side of Paradise*, 51; Turnbull, *Fitzgerald*, 56, 60, 68, 72; Fitzgerald, *Ledger*, 170, 171.

42. Mizener, *Far Side of Paradise*, 48, 50.

43. Mizener, *Far Side of Paradise*, 48, 49, 64, 101, 106, 321n; Bruccoli, Smith, and Kerr, eds., *Romantic Egoists*, 26.

44. William F. Peet, *The Beginnings of Golf in Saint Paul and the Early History of the Town and Country Club*, 1–3 (St. Paul, 1930); Summersby to author, November 20, 1976; *Town and Country Club, Saint Paul, Minnesota: Its Government, Organization, and Membership*, 37–47 (St. Paul, 1915).

45. Bruccoli, Smith, and Kerr, eds., *Romantic Egoists*, 26; Mizener, *Far Side of Paradise*, 47–50.

46. Mizener, *Far Side of Paradise*, 13; Sandeen, *Historic Summit Avenue*, 94; Fitzgerald, *Ledger*, 169.

47. Fitzgerald, *Ledger*, 169; Mizener, *Far Side of Paradise*, 47, 53.

48. Mizener, *Far Side of Paradise*, 57; Fitzgerald, *Ledger*, 170.

49. Mizener, *Far Side of Paradise*, 53–57; Fitzgerald, *Ledger*, 170. Fitzgerald spent the summer of 1915 visiting his friend Charles W. ("Sap") Donahoe on his Montana ranch.

50. Mizener, *Far Side of Paradise*, 64–66; Fitzgerald, *Ledger*, 170, 171, 172.

51. Mizener, *Far Side of Paradise*, 13; Fitzgerald, *Ledger*, 173.

52. Fitzgerald, *Ledger*, 2, 172; Mizener, *Far Side of Paradise*, 70–72.

53. Fitzgerald, *Ledger*, 173; Mizener, *Far Side of Paradise*, 73, 74–81.

54. Mizener, *Far Side of Paradise*, 82; Fitzgerald, *Ledger*, 173.

55. Mizener, *Far Side of Paradise*, 83.

56. Turnbull, *Fitzgerald*, 96–98.

57. John Kuehl and Jackson R. Bryer, eds., *Dear Scott/Dear Max: The Fitzgerald-Perkins Correspondence*, 17 (New York, 1971).

58. Mizener, *Far Side of Paradise*, 86; Fitzgerald, *Ledger*, 174.

59. Kuehl and Bryer, eds., *Dear Scott/Dear Max*, 21; Fitzgerald, *Ledger*, 174; Mizener, *Far Side of Paradise*, 87.

60. Mizener, *Far Side of Paradise*, 89.

61. Sandeen, *Historic Summit Avenue*, 91–93; Holbert and Holmquist, *50 Twin City Landmarks*, 15.

62. John DeQuedville Briggs was headmaster of St. Paul

Academy from 1914 to 1950; Mizener, in *Far Side of Paradise*, 86, is wrong when he says Briggs was not yet headmaster. Briggs was for a time even more peripatetic than his novelist friend, living in half a dozen different places in as many years—among them, the University Club, 501 Grand Avenue (the Ames's house), 478 Ashland, and 550 Summit, in addition to 513 Summit. For information here and below see Fitch, *Some Aspects of SPA/SS*, 3, 4; St. Paul city directories, 1915–22; interview with Elizabeth Ames Jackson and Norris Dean Jackson.

63. For this and information following, see Robert D. Clark to author, April 24, 1976; interview with Joseph H. Watson, former clerk at Grotto Pharmacy, 1977; Mizener, *Far Side of Paradise*, 85.

64. On Father Barron and the information below, see Turnbull, *Fitzgerald*, 98, 128; Mizener, *Far Side of Paradise*, 85; Fitzgerald, *Ledger*, 172; interview with Msgr. Francis Gilligan of the Cathedral of St. Paul and Father Clyde Eddy of St. Paul Seminary; obituary in *Catholic Bulletin* (St. Paul), April 22, 1939. p. 1.

65. Mizener, *Far Side of Paradise*, 133; Mackey J. Thompson (Jr.) to author, November 15, 1976.

66. *St. Paul Daily News*, August 16, p. 11, September 25, 1921, feature section, p. 6; Bruccoli, Smith, and Kerr, eds., *Romantic Egoists*, 92.

67. Thompson to author, November 15, 1976; *St. Paul Daily News*, October 4, 1921, p. 10; Fitzgerald, *Ledger*, 175, 176.

68. Fitzgerald and Zelda Fitzgerald, "Show Mr. and Mrs. F. to Number—," in Wilson, ed., *Crack-Up*, 42.

69. Mizener, *Far Side of Paradise*, 137; Fitzgerald to Edmund Wilson, January 24, 1922, in Wilson, ed., *Crack-Up*, 257; Fitzgerald, *Ledger*, 176, 177; Kuehl and Bryer, eds., *Dear Scott/Dear Max*, 41–43.

70. Robert E. Hoag, "The Hotels of St. Paul," 8, 116 (St. Paul, 1975), typed manuscript, copy in MHS; St. Paul city directory, 1920, p. 6; *Grand Gazettte*, September–October, 1973, p. 1. The wooden deck of the rooftop garden and small kitchen burned in 1945 and was never rebuilt, according to owner Thomond O'Brien, August 30, 1978.

71. *Minneapolis Tribune*, February 16, 1978, p. 1; *St. Paul Dispatch*, February 16, 1978, p. 1; interview with Peggy Faricy, March 2004.

72. Mizener, *Far Side of Paradise*, 136; Fitzgerald, *Ledger*, 176; Kuehl and Bryer, eds., *Dear Scott/Dear Max*, 44–59. Sarah and Cecelia Kalman had gone abroad, fortuitously leaving the house available to the Fitzgeralds.

73. Turnbull, *Fitzgerald,* 128; Mizener, *Far Side of Paradise,* 134; Kuehl and Bryer, eds., *Dear Scott Dear Max,* 44–59.

74. Turnbull, *Fitzgerald,* 128; St. Paul city directories, 1922–25.

75. Mizener, *Far Side of Paradise,* 137, 148; Turnbull, *Fitzgerald,* 132; Fitzgerald, *Ledger,* 176.

76. St. Paul city directories, 1918–22; interview with James Taylor Dunn, June 1978.

77. *University Club of St. Paul, 1915,* 3 (directory of members), copy in MHS; Griggs to author, November 20, 1976; Fitzgerald, *Ledger,* 176.

78. Turnbull, *Fitzgerald,* 69.

79. *St. Paul Daily Dirge,* January 13, 1922, copy in MHS.

80. Interview with Peggy Faricy, March 2004.

81. Fitzgerald, *Ledger,* 165; Robert Clark to author, April 24, May 17, 1976.

82. Mizener, *Far Side of Paradise,* 27; Turnbull, *Fitzgerald,* 43; Bruccoli, Smith, and Kerr, eds., *Romantic Egoists,* 18, 19; Fitzgerald, *Ledger,* 167.

83. Fitzgerald, *Ledger,* 168; Mizener, *Far Side of Paradise,* 45; Turnbull, *Fitzgerald,* 53.

84. Read to author, January 8, 1977; Mizener, *Far Side of Paradise,* 49; "Winter Dreams," in Cowley, ed., *Stories of Fitzgerald,* 127–145.

85. Fitzgerald, *Ledger,* 4, 176; Kuehl and Bryer, eds., *Dear Scott/Dear Max,* 60–62; Mizener, *Far Side of Paradise,* 148; Turnbull, *Fitzgerald,* 133.

86. Fitzgerald, *Ledger,* 176; Mizener, *Far Side of Paradise,* 148, 149; Mrs. Lewis to author, January 1, 1977.

87. For this and information below, see interview with Gene J. Marshall, manager of White Bear Yacht Club; Drake et al., *White Bear Yacht Club,* 137.

A Guide to F. Scott Fitzgerald's St. Paul was designed and set in type by Percolator, Minneapolis, who used Stone Serif, designed by Sumner Stone in 1987, for the text type. The book was printed by Transcontinental Printing, Peterborough, Ontario.

ALSO AVAILABLE FROM THE MINNESOTA HISTORICAL SOCIETY PRESS

The Minnesota Book of Days:
An Almanac of State History
by Tony Greiner

A fun and fascinating day-by-day account of Minnesota history, chronicling important events, famous firsts, notable individuals, and interesting incidents. A perfect gift for any fan of Minnesota history and trivia.

$13.95, paper, ISBN 0-87351-416-5

Minnesota History along the Highways:
A Guide to Historic Markers and Sites
Compiled by Sarah P. Rubinstein

A handy travel guide to more than 254 historic markers, 60 geologic markers, and 29 state historic monuments throughout the state.

$13.95, paper, ISBN 0-87351-456-4

The National Register of Historic Places
in Minnesota: A Guide
Compiled by Mary Ann Nord

A county-by-county guide to Minnesota's more than 1,500 holdings on the National Register of Historic Places, the country's official list of historic properties.

$13.95, paper, ISBN 0-87351-448-3

The Pocket Guide to Minnesota Place Names
by Michael Fedo

The pocket version of the authoritative *Minnesota Place Names,* 3rd Edition. This handy guide is the perfect companion for anyone who travels the highways and waterways of the North Star state.

$11.95, paper, ISBN 0-87351-424-6

Six Feet Under: A Graveyard Guide to Minnesota
By Stu Thornley

A haunting tour of the final resting places of famous and infamous Minnesotans throughout their home state, with side trips to include some who ended up elsewhere.

$14.95, paper, ISBN 0-87351-514-5

JOIN THE MINNESOTA HISTORICAL SOCIETY TODAY! IT'S THE BEST DEAL IN HISTORY!

The Minnesota Historical Society is the nation's premier state historical society. Founded in 1849, the Society collects, preserves, and tells the story of Minnesota's past through innovative museum exhibits, extensive collections and libraries, educational programs, historic sites, and book and magazine publishing. Membership support is vital to the Society's ability to serve its ever-broadening and increasingly diverse public with programs and services that are educational, engaging, and entertaining.

What are the benefits of membership?

Members enjoy:

- A subscription to the quarterly magazine *Minnesota History;*
- *Member News* newsletter and events calendar;
- Unlimited free admission to the Society's 25 historic sites;
- Discounts on purchases from the Minnesota Historical Society Press and on other purchases and services in our museum stores, library, Café Minnesota, and much more;
- Reciprocal benefits at more than 70 historical organizations and museums in over 40 states through Time Travelers; and
- Satisfaction of knowing your membership helps support the Society's programs.

Membership fees/categories:

- $65 Household (2 adults and children under 18 in same household)
- $45 Senior Household (age 65+ for 2 adults)
- $55 Individual (1 adult)
- $45 Senior Individual (age 65+ for 1 adult)
- $125 Associate
- $250 Contributing
- $500 Sustaining
- $1,000 North Star Circle

Join by phone or e-mail. To order by phone, call 651-296-0332 (TTY 651-282-6073) or e-mail membership@mnhs.org. Benefits extend one year from date of joining.